THE GREATER FEAR

SPIRITUAL POWER TO OVERCOME UNHEALTHY FEARS

———

2ND EDITION

Brad Jones

With introduction by Dr. C. Wayne Childers
and additional chapter by Bret Ellard, LPC.

© 2018 CHILDERS-ELLARD

Unless otherwise noted, scripture quotations noted NASB are from the NEW AMERICAN STANDARD BIBLE. © The Lockman Foundation 1960, 1962, 1963, 1968, 1971, 1972, 1973, 1975, 1977. Used by permission. (www.Lockman.org)

Copyright 2003 Brad Jones

All rights reserved. No part of this publication may be reproduced, stored in a retrieval system or transmitted in any form or by any means (electronic, mechanical, photocopy, recording, or otherwise) without prior permission of the copyright owner.

1st Edition Printed and published by Church Strengthening Ministry of the Foreign Mission Board, SBC, Inc., Makati City, Philippines

2nd Edition Published 2018 by Childers-Ellard with permission from the authors estate.

ISBN 9781724139450

Dedication

To my son Russell, my chief encourager,
with thanks to my sister Carol
who improved my style of writing.

Contents

New Introduction 6
An Invitation 8

Part 1- The Greater Fear 11
'Twas Grace that Taught My Heart to Fear and Grace My Fears Relieved

1 - Crossing the Threshold of Courage 12
2 - The Greater Fear 17
3 - From God's Heart to Yours 48

Part 2 - Finding Your Way 59
How Precious did that Grace Appear the Hour I First Believed

4 - The One Who Showed the Way 60
5 - How We Lost Our Way 71
6 - Unlocking Heaven's Treasure 88

Part 3 - More than a Feeling 103
'Tis Grace Hath Brought Me Safe Thus Far and Grace Will Lead Me Home

7 - Reverence in Our Hearts 104
8 - Reverence in Our Homes 111
9 - Reverence in the Church 120
10 - Reverence in the Workplace 134
11 - Reverence in Our Relationships 145

An Exhortation 165
For further reflection:
   Study Questions 168

Introduction to the Second Edition

The Greater Fear, by Dr. R. Bradley Jones, first edition, has been read and reread by individuals and used by churches, religious organizations, counselors and missions leaders since its publication in 2003. In 2006 Dr. Jones died unexpectedly in Oklahoma City at the age of 55. His ministry continued through this little book.

It has been translated into Hindi, Tagalog, Cebuano, and Spanish and has been used in India, the Philippines, Haiti, Mexico, Vietnam, Japan, Thailand and Singapore.

This edition updates the content and adds a chapter by Bret Ellard, LPC on using it with clients as a counseling resource. Ellard is a Christian Counselor in private practice in Shawnee, Oklahoma. He has been in practice for more than 30 years and has used this book with clients suffering with various fears.

I was Brad's roommate in Seminary and we were close friends and confidantes since 1974. I was on his board of directors at the time of his death with Keith Johnson and Paul Moore. We continued his training mission, through local leadership, in India and the Philippines until 2017 when the mission was complete.

Bret Ellard and I are reprinting this book for our use in churches, conferences and with individuals. We are grateful for the support of Brad's son Dr. Russell Jones and the two board members mentioned. We want the ideas Brad captured from his Bible Study to continue to bless others.

Sincerely,

Dr. C. Wayne Childers
Former Director of Church Renewal International

An Invitation

When Joan, a lady in her early thirties, entered my office she was obviously distraught. "Pastor, I'm scared and don't know what to do." She had an appointment with her doctor in two days. Earlier in the week she had discovered a suspicious lump in one of her breasts. Immediately she had been gripped with the fear that she had cancer and soon would be dead. This was not a new fear for Joan. Her mother had died of cancer at an early age. For years Joan had been hounded by a sense of dread which lived just below the level of her conscious thinking, the nagging whispered thought that her life would be cut short by the same awful disease. It seemed that everything she had feared was now becoming an unnerving reality. I showed her Proverbs 14:26. *"In the fear of the LORD there is strong confidence,"* and asked, "Would you permit me to pray with you that the Lord will give you this blessed fear so that you have confidence to face the days ahead?" She quickly went to her knees and I asked God to bestow the fear that brings courage and to show Himself strong on her behalf.

The next day I received a phone call from Joan. "I just had to tell you what has happened to me." She sounded very excited. I thought she was about to tell me that the lump was gone. "Oh no, the lump is still there," she said. "I still have the appointment with my doctor tomorrow and I may have cancer. But an amazing thing has happened. That paralyzing fear is gone! I may have to face some difficult days ahead. I don't know. But I do know that I can face what comes because God is with me whatever happens."

It turned out that there was no malignancy. But there was a change in Joan. She had discovered a powerful truth. There is a kind of fear that produces boldness in one's heart. *"In the fear of the Lord there is strong confidence."* It sounds like a contradiction. How can fear bring confidence? One of my seminary teachers, Jack MacGorman, said, "The man who has lost his fear of God will be subject by default to a thousand lesser fears." I believe God has written a law into the heart of man. The principle is this. The greater fear will always break the power of the lesser fear in your life.

We live in an age of fear. The attack on the World Trade Center on September 11, 2001 grabbed the attention of the world and affirmed the necessity for an international war on terrorism. Our leaders have declared war on those who want to use fear against us. But who will declare war on the fear itself? The battle against fear is not a new one. All of us know what it is to wrestle with fear. I am glad you have picked up this book because it invites you to accept an amazingly powerful resource available in the fight against unhealthy fears. And it may surprise you that the key to winning this battle lies in embracing the one fear you don't want to lose. Countless heroes of the past have utilized what you will learn in these pages to win the battle over fear. This old truth is bringing a new resolve to thousands who are confronted with the need to find courage in the face of fear. Unhealthy fears are hard to fight on our own. That is why I am praying that this book will increase your understanding of how God fights for you. I invite you to embrace the healthy fear that brings freedom from destructive anxieties that otherwise will dominate your response to life. When you call upon God to give you His holy fear, boldness comes with the answer. To cultivate the greater fear is to conquer the lesser ones.

Part 1
The Greater Fear

'Twas Grace that Taught My Heart to Fear and Grace My Fears Relieved

Chapter One

Crossing the Threshold of Courage

The Answer

I did not know that God was opening my heart and sliding His scalpel deep into my soul. Weakness swallowed me. Crumpling to my knees on the chapel carpet, I feared I would either lose my mind or my life. This room had held wonderful memories, but seemed so fearful now. For eight good years I had pastored a growing suburban congregation. Fourteen like hearted people had started with a God given dream. Through toil, laughter, tears and joy, we watched our dream blossom into a reality we could see and taste and feel. But on that day, August 10, 1985, I was dealing with more than a dream. I was pressed against a Presence that overshadowed my hopes and my hurts. Trembling grabbed my heart. In a moment I was undone. And re-done.

As I look back on it I find it strange that I did not immediately connect this experience with an incident that had happened two months earlier. But how could I have? I had not even understood the prayer, much less the answer.

The Prayer

It was the first week of June in the seacoast city of Aomori, Japan. Aomori is a picturesque city on the northern coast of Honshu. I was engaged in a speaking tour and had been given the use of an upstairs guestroom in a small church. While I prayed one morning, the Spirit of God spoke to my heart. Although there was no audible voice the words were clear. "I want you to ask Me to teach you to fear Me." The thought stunned me. I called, "What, Lord?" Again the words pounded in my heart, "I want you to ask Me to teach you to fear Me." The idea that God was speaking in this fashion was frightening in itself. Yes, I knew Proverbs 1:7 says, *"the fear of the Lord is the beginning of wisdom."*

But it suddenly seemed much too real and much too close.

I could not bring myself to utter such a prayer. After all, I loved God. Did not perfect love cast out fear? I had spent much of my adult life trying to conquer fears through faith in God. How could it be that my Father was now calling me to fear? I enjoyed such sweet fellowship at His hand. Was I now to find terrors there?

Despite swirling questions within, there hung an unshakable conviction that I had heard from God. I knew that disobedience would damage the divine fellowship that had become precious to me. I also saw that a glib mouthing of such a prayer without sincerity of heart was unthinkable. Two days of wrestling passed before I called to heaven. "Father, teach me to fear You." There! I had managed it. I possessed little understanding of the consequences and practically no enthusiasm. But I was full of sincerity. "Besides," I reasoned, "if God is doing something in my life, I can trust Him. No doubt this will turn out for my good." *So why was my heart still aflutter?*

I braced myself, but heavenly fireworks were noticeably absent. A peace descended and I resumed my overseas assignment. Upon returning home I found myself slipping into a restless sense of spiritual bankruptcy. In this dry time, I had all but forgotten the prayer made halfway around the world. Then, in the chapel, I found that God had not forgotten the prayer nor had He neglected to answer!

Crossing the Threshold of Courage

In the aftermath of the chapel surgery, I began to notice a change in my life. Having tasted the fear of the Lord, I started shedding some other fears. For years destructive trepidations had dictated my response to life's open doors. But I did not know it. In fact, I most certainly would have bristled had you suggested that I was driven by fear. I think unholy fear was such a close companion that I had long since lost awareness of its hold.

Sometimes you must taste freedom before you realize the extent of your bondage. Has this happened to you? You spend time inside your house and then go outdoors where you take in some fresh air. When you return inside you are assaulted by a stale, clammy odor. The smell was there all the time, but you did not detect it before. That's the way it was with my fears. I had to get a little distance from them before I recognized how tightly they had held me.

I had not set out to conquer these fears, but they were gone. Without planning to do so, I crossed the threshold of courage and stepped into the fresh atmosphere of an adventure that continues today. It was the first of many blessings I was to discover awaiting me when my heart became awakened to a higher Fear.

Chapter Two

The Greater Fear

"In the fear of the Lord there is strong confidence"
Proverbs 14:26

The Fear that Brings Courage

Let us suppose that the end of the month is nearing and you are paying your bills. As each check is written your bank balance gets lower. Finally, you come to the last invoice to be paid, your water bill. It is not a large amount of money, but when you note the balance in your checkbook you discover that you do not have enough to pay the bill. Some anxiety creeps into your heart. You begin to think about your financial future. There is no immediate prospect of an increase in family income, but expenses keep growing. This month it is the water bill. What will it be next month? "If something doesn't change," you reason, "there could be a financial disaster down the road." Fear is rising. Just then your phone rings. When you answer, you hear, "This is Regional Hospital calling. Your family has been involved in an automobile accident and is being treated in our emergency room. Come quickly." You hang up the phone, grab your car keys, race out the door, and speed down the street toward the hospital. At this point worry about a water bill has no chance of grabbing your thoughts, not because you stood on a Divine promise of provision or exercised strong faith, but because something bigger has pushed that fear out of a position to bother you. You have been gripped by a bigger fear.

Or imagine this scene. You and I are walking along a railroad track. We come to a place where the track crosses a river. Together we step out onto the trestle and start across the river. About halfway across I point out how inviting the water looks and suggest that we go for a swim. This bothers you, but before you can voice your objection I dive off the bridge into the water below. Now you are really nervous. Peering into the water thirty feet below, you wonder what has become of me. In a few seconds I resurface, laughing and calling for you to join me. Your fear mounts as you stare into the swirling water beneath you. You try to muster the courage to make the leap, but you just can't do it. At that precise moment you hear a sound. It's a train! You realize that you can't make it to either end of the trestle before the locomotive reaches you. What will you do? You look at the river. You look at the train. Just as the engine reaches the edge of the river the whistle blasts a warning. Every nerve in your body screams for a reaction and you leap off the trestle into the water below.

How were you able to overcome your fear of jumping into the river? It was actually quite simple, wasn't it? You did not have to do anything to overcome that fear. Once you were gripped by a greater fear, plunging into the river seemed like the easy thing to do. Remember the principle? *The greater fear will always break the power of a lesser fear in your life.* Now let's see how this principle applies to the fear of the Lord.

In the first chapter of Exodus, Pharaoh commanded the midwives Shiphrah and Puah to kill all male babies born to the Hebrews in Goshen. The people that Joseph brought into Egypt were becoming very numerous and posed a threat to the power structures of the kingdom. Pharaoh's murderous policy was designed to keep the Hebrews in a position of weakness and servitude. Surprisingly, however, Shiphrah and Puah disobeyed Pharaoh's instructions. Certainly they must have understood that refusal to carry out the royal dictate would mean the death penalty for them. Nevertheless, they found the courage to defy Pharaoh and spare the lives of the baby boys they delivered, among them the infant Moses. A careful reading of the passage reveals the source of their courage. Verse 17 says, *"But the midwives feared God, and did not do as the king of Egypt had commanded them, but let the boys live."* They had seen Pharaoh's power and knew the consequences of disobedience to him. Ordinarily such knowledge would have been enough to scare them into submission, except for one thing-they had a greater fear in their hearts. They had glimpsed a greater King than Pharaoh. Their attention was on One whose awesomeness caused Pharaoh's power to pale by comparison. The holy fear of the Lord rooted out any chance that the fear of Pharaoh would dominate their lives. It gave them courage to do what was right.

The greater fear, the fear of the Lord, broke the power of the lesser fear of Pharaoh in their lives.

What is the Fear of the Lord?

The fear of the Lord is more than a concept to be conveyed from one mind to another. Strictly speaking it is evoked more than taught and awakened more than analyzed. It is highly reasonable, yet it goes farther than reason alone can take us. There are emotions that attend it, but it is much more than a feeling. Biblical descriptions of it focus on how it acts more than on what it is. As the story of Shiphrah and Puah illustrates, the fear of the Lord causes us to affirm His supreme majesty and respond in reverent obedience to His righteousness despite fearful circumstances.

Fighting fears with Fear

Few of us are called to defy a Pharaoh, but all of us live with fearful circumstances and the promise holds for us as it did for Shiphrah and Puah: grounding our lives in the greater fear of the Lord neutralizes the lesser fears that often haunt us.

Randy approached me after I had spoken at a gathering in Alabama. He had just received word that his military unit was being sent overseas. "Brad, I love my country," he said, "and I'm glad to serve in the military. But I have a problem. In order to get to my assignment, I have to travel by airplane. Flying scares me to death. You said the healthy fear of God breaks the power of unhealthy fears. That's what I need.

Would you pray with me?" As we knelt together, Randy requested that the fear of the Lord be planted in his heart. As the weeks passed I wondered about Randy. Then I got a call from his pastor. After discussing a number of things he said, "By the way, I heard from Randy today and he gave me a message for you. He said that he has flown almost every plane the government has in service without a moment's trouble. I hope that message makes sense to you." Indeed it did. And it makes sense to me that embracing the fear of God is a great way to shed those nagging fears that hold us back from courageously facing each new day.

The desk clerk at the motel where I was staying called the room and asked if I could come to the lobby. She had something important to tell me. I had met Tracy two days earlier. I was in town to lead a conference in her church. She was a young mother of two preschoolers. "I am so glad you could come," she said. "I just had to tell you what God has done in my life. Last night I went to bed at 10:30 and slept all night. It was wonderful!" While I was glad Tracy had slept well, I did not understand her excitement until she explained, "My husband works out of town several days each week. When he's gone I'm always too afraid to go to bed. I stay up until I am so exhausted that I can't help but sleep. Only then do I go to bed and often it's two or three in the morning. If my husband's at home I'm fine, but when he's gone, I'm too afraid to sleep. When you explained that the fear of God brings courage, I knew that's what I needed. I prayed for the holy fear of the Lord and I think I have lost my fear of being alone at night."

As Shiphrah, Puah, Randy and Tracy know, God has provided a way to win the battle over unhealthy fears. The possession of the healthy fear of the Lord brings freedom from fears that would otherwise dominate our thoughts and paralyze our lives.

In the following pages I will discuss five common fears we face:
the fear of exposure
the fear of man
the fear of failure
the fear of rejection
the fear of death

In every case we'll see how the fear of God overcomes unholy and destructive fears. Indeed, the way to conquer each of these unhealthy fears is to cultivate the holy fear of the Lord.

1 - The Fear of Exposure

"They will begin TO SAY TO THE MOUNTAINS, 'FALL ON US,' AND TO THE HILLS, 'COVER US.'" Luke 23:30

The first mention of fear in Scripture is found in Genesis 3:10. Adam and Eve had just disobeyed God and eaten forbidden fruit. With the entrance of sin into the created order came something man had never experienced before. A destructive fear gripped his soul. Adam and Eve knew that the Lord would be coming to enjoy fellowship with them in the beautiful coolness of the garden. They had always cherished this sweet nearness, but today there was no joy in the thought of walking with God. Dread wrapped its icy fingers around their hearts. In panic they plunged into the dense foliage, trying desperately to cover themselves with branches, dirt, rocks... anything that would hide the condition of their hearts from the holy gaze of God.

That day they found out what many have since learned. You cannot hide from God. Reluctantly, trembling before His holiness, they stepped forward to confess their fear. *"I heard the sound of Thee in the garden, and I was afraid ..."* Genesis 3:10. They did not confess their sin. They were still trying to hide that. They did acknowledge the terror that drove them to seek distance from the Lord. This urge to flee was not the holy fear of God. It was the unholy fear of exposure. Their sin had separated them from God, even though they stood before Him. They were physically in the presence of God and yet infinitely removed from the intimacy with Him that had once nourished them and made paradise out of their garden.

Since that day men and women of every generation have feared exposure of the shame that lies within the human heart. We cover it, mask it, deny it. In fact we have become masters at the art of deception. We will not allow others too close, lest we become uncovered. We even try to fool ourselves into believing our own denials. The most tragic consequence of this fear of exposure is that it encourages flight from God. We withdraw from intimacy with Him lest what we have hidden becomes known.

How can we rid ourselves of this destructive dread that distances us from the Lord? A clue to resolving the dilemma can be found in Acts 19:17-18. The church in Ephesus had been started almost three years earlier by the Apostle Paul. The believers had been growing numerically and spiritually. They had witnessed tremendous miracles and were blossoming in the grace being poured into their lives. Still, they had a deadly phobia that was keeping them from freedom and fullness and joy. They were afraid to be open with each other. To be sure they carefully composed themselves to project the message, "There's nothing wrong here." Yet, they were hiding the truth. Behind Sunday smiles these early Christians concealed gross iniquities. They played a dangerous game that is common among believers today-the game of hypocrisy. Hypocrisy is the attempt to appear to be better than we really are. Members of the church in Ephesus were trying to look fully committed to Christ while they clung to secret sins that included the practice of magical arts to try to ward off the power of Satan and his demons.

Then, something happened that unlocked their hearts from the fear of exposure. *"Many also of those who had believed kept coming, confessing and disclosing their practices"* (verse 18). They started revealing what they had always taken great pains to hide.

What miracle brought this cleansing release to the people of God? I believe the answer can be found in verse 17: *"and fear fell upon them all."* This was not an ordinary fear and quickly produced some extraordinary results. It did not send them into hiding or generate panic and confusion. Nor did it inhibit the progress of the church, as we might expect fear to do. Rather it caused them to erupt in praise to God and to become transparent before one another. As a consequence of this fear *".. .the word of the Lord was growing mightily and prevailing"* (verse 20).

The people rid themselves of the magic paraphernalia they had secretly used to manage their fears. They no longer needed to manage what holy fear had conquered. Freed from the weight of unholy fears, the church boldly took its place as a proactive instrument in the hands of God.

The fear of God was the match that ignited revival fires in the Ephesian church. We know this was the holy fear of God because of the behavior it produced *"...by the fear of the LORD men depart from evil"* (Proverbs 16:6 KJV). When the fear of God filled their hearts, the Ephesians began to despise sin more than they feared exposure. They threw off their masks. Instead of keeping their distance from God and other believers, they now distanced themselves from the sin that had insidiously lurked behind their smiles for so long.

I believe the fear of exposure robs many people of the healing touch of God upon their lives. While I was teaching in a Canadian church one spring, a young lady experienced release from a sense of shame that she had carried for years. She had hidden her history as a victim of sexual abuse, trying to bury her pain by being a good wife and faithful Christian. The constant fear that her past might become known kept her in turmoil. Peace of mind and heart was impossible because of this hidden fear. When she was convinced from Scripture that the fear of the Lord was a blessing God intended for her, she embraced it eagerly. Courage to face her old fear began to build in her heart. Soon she found the strength to reveal her secret to her husband and a few dose Christian friends. The acceptance they gave her and the joy that followed set her on a course of healing and released her from the paralyzing dread that had enslaved her. The holy fear of the Lord broke the power of the fear of exposure, set her free from the bondage of her past and provided her with a powerful testimony with which she has been able to help others.

Exposure is the first step to covering our sin. It is only natural for us to want our sin covered. King David said, *"How blessed is he whose transgression is forgiven, Whose sin is covered!"* (Psalm 32:1). God also wants to cover our sin, but there is a big difference between man's attempts to cover sin and God's plan to cover it. Man's method is to cover sin with secrecy. He will go to great lengths to hide what is lodged in his heart.

Secrecy only causes the shame to fester However, secrecy only causes the shame to fester and drives the deadly defilement deeper into the soul, where it infects the core of his being. God wants to cover the wound of sin with the healing balm of grace. For that to happen, He must first uncover our hearts. Then He brings that exposed heart to the cross of Christ, where the wound that sin inflicted is washed. The fountain of Christ's shed blood is the only place where a sin-blackened heart can be washed white. Then that sin is forever covered by the forgiveness of our loving God.

I was teaching a group of several hundred pastors in the Philippines on the subject of the fear of the Lord. After one of the sessions a young man approached me and asked that I pray for him. He told me that he was having an affair with another man's wife. He knew what he was doing was bringing a destructive consequence into several lives. He felt ashamed and trapped. He said he had not wanted to come to the seminar, but was comforted to learn that the holy fear of the Lord is an expression of God's grace. It had given him the courage to share his secret sin with me and to ask for help. A heavy burden lifted as he found himself able to expose to another what he had spent incredible amounts of energy trying to hide. He followed the biblical injunction to *"Confess your faults one to another and pray for one another that you may be healed"* (James 5:16).

Many of us have something in our lives that we are hiding. Fear of exposure can be a very powerful force. It can cause us to bury sin deep within our hearts and to believe that there is no way out. We feel condemned to live a double life. But when the holy fear of the Lord does its work within us, we are freed from the prison of hypocrisy. We find the courage to face our shame.

Fear of exposure can be like a child's misgiving when presenting a scraped knee to his mother for doctoring. "Will it sting?" he asks when she approaches with disinfectant in hand.

Sometimes his fear of the medicine will even lead him to deny his wound. "It's all better now, mommy." At this point a loving mother will assist the child in overcoming his fear, so that healing can take place.

Do not be afraid of the stinging touch of God's healing hand. You can open your heart and show him the full extent of your sin. If you are afraid of the exposure, ask for the holy fear of God. It is your Father's gift to help you come out of hiding and enter the place of healing.

2 - The Fear of Man
"Now Obadiah feared the LORD greatly." 1 Kings 18:3

Do you know someone who bullies others into submission by fear and intimidation? Queen Jezebel was just such a bully. She had married into power by becoming the wife of Ahab, King of Israel, and immediately made it clear throughout the kingdom that it would be her way or the highway in religious practices. She had grown up worshiping the god of the Sidonians and would never convert to the God of Israel. Instead, she insisted that everyone adopt her god. She even had 850 prophets of Baal on the palace payroll to see to it that things were done her way. She had a simple way of ending the career of any preacher who opposed her. She removed his head.

It was in this climate of intimidation and persecution that Obadiah lived. Obadiah, a worshiper of Jehovah, was faced with a dilemma. Would he compromise his service to God or risk the wrath of Jezebel? Many a believer has since stood where Obadiah stood. Perhaps the choice is not as stark or the consequences as grave, but a price is required of anyone who wishes to maintain faithfulness to God when the mainstream of society is taking a different course. The kingdoms of this world are not always kind to those whose loyalties are to heaven's kingdom.

We know little about Obadiah, but what we are told is very instructive. He was highly placed in the royal administration. 1 Kings 18:3-4 tells us that he was over the household of Ahab and Jezebel. When Jezebel's murderous policy began to be enforced against the prophets of God, it became apparent that Obadiah was either going to have to betray his Lord or betray Jezebel. To Obadiah's credit he chose integrity over expediency. He risked his position and his life by hiding 100 prophets from Jezebel, secreting them in two caves and smuggling food and water to them. Obviously such action put him in great peril. Yet, he was able to overcome the fear of what the Queen's men would do to him should he be caught. The Biblical account clearly links his courageous plan of resistance to the fact that *"Obadiah feared the LORD greatly"* (verse 3). Obadiah learned that a healthy fear of God enables us to courageously face fearful circumstances without compromise.

Lou was a middle-aged lady who lived in an upper middle class neighborhood. She and her husband still had their two youngest daughters at home with them.

She approached me one morning and said, "Pastor, you told us that if we would embrace the fear of God, it would break the power of unholy fears in our lives. Well, let me tell you what happened to me. I asked the Lord to give me His holy fear at church. Then I went home. That night I prepared for bed and went through my normal routine of checking and locking all the doors and windows before climbing into bed. Normally, after retiring, I lie awake thinking, 'Did I lock that kitchen screen?' So I get up and check the screen again. While I am up I recheck all the other doors and windows. Sometimes I rise three or four times a night to make sure the house is secure. This pattern has gone on for years. But it was different the night I prayed for the fear of God. Once in bed I went right to sleep. The next several nights I locked the doors before retiring and again went quickly to sleep. Then it dawned on me. I wasn't getting up repeatedly during the night to check my locks. No longer was I unreasonably anxious about the possibility of a break-in. I still lock the doors at night, but I have lost the fear that cost me so much sleep over the years."

Jesus instructed us not to fear those who can kill the body but after that have nothing more that they can do to us. Immediately on the heels of that injunction He gave another command. He said that we were to

> **Embracing the fear of God can actually extinguish the fear of man.**

fear God whose power extends beyond life and death. *" ... yes, I tell you, fear Him!"* (See Luke 12:4-5). Amazingly, it is obedience to the latter command that can help us to find the courage to obey the former. Embracing the fear of God can actually extinguish the fear of man.

I have a friend who is a pastor in Asia. When he was still a young man a wave of persecution arose in the area where he lived. A number of pastors he knew were killed because of their faith in Jesus Christ. Understandably my friend found himself gripped by a paralyzing fear. He wanted to run and hide, but God gave him courage to remain steadfast and not deny his Lord or his calling. He told me that while he meditated on the Lord's command to fear God, he became so aware of God's strength that his fear of those persecuting the church no longer overwhelmed him. From that day to this he has boldly served our Lord and His church as a leader among evangelical Christians in that part of the world. An incident in the Old Testament describes how another man discovered courage in the face of religious persecution.

Nehemiah lived over twenty-four hundred years ago. He was a descendant of the Jews in exile in Babylon. He was also the personal cupbearer to the Persian ruler Artaxerxes. Upon learning that the city walls of Jerusalem were in ruins, he obtained permission to lead an expedition to repair them. Once Nehemiah and his crew began the work, their enemies, determined to stop them, sent repeated warnings that blood would flow if they continued the project. Nehemiah saw that his men were losing heart, so he took action. *"When I saw their fear, I rose and spoke to the nobles, the officials, and the rest of the people: 'Do not be afraid of them; remember the Lord who is great and awesome,..."* (See Nehemiah 4:14). Nehemiah was convinced that if his men contemplated the strength and power of God, that the strength of those threatening them would seem weak by comparison. Sure enough, encouraged by the knowledge of the greatness of their God, these Israelites were able to withstand the demands of their enemies. The work continued and was completed with astonishing speed. Nehemiah, whose name means the Lord is consolation, recognized that the awesomeness of God does indeed hearten those who face intimidation from men who oppose the work God gives His people to do.

3 - Fear of Failure

"Then Moses answered and said, 'What if they will not believe

Fear of failure can diminish you.

me, or listen to what I say?"'" Exodus 4:1a

Fear of failure can diminish you. In the case of Moses it produced a marvelous plan God had for him. God called him to the high privilege of delivering a nation from bondage. However, he had already made some efforts in regard to this business of deliverance and the results had been disastrous. As a consequence, Moses was afraid to try. His initial response was, "No, thank you. I'd be better off hiding on the side of this mountain than tackling a venture that is sure to fail."

The reality of past failure or the prospect of future failure has immobilized more people than you or I can count. The believer who won't talk to her neighbor about her faith for fear that she will be asked a question she cannot answer, or the businessman who won't finance a heavenly cause because he fears the loss of his reserve funds, or the young man who won't ask the girl he likes for a date because the last girl turned him down all have one thing in common: they let their fear of failure shape their lives. How much better it is when we let faith—not fear— determine our course of action, and how reassuring it is to know that the fear of the Lord is fully adequate to conquer this debilitating phobia.

I watched the school basketball teams on a regular basis and noticed that one of the girls exhibited a strong measure of skill on the court but usually wore a worried expression on her face while playing. She heard me speak on the fear of God and came to me after a service to talk about it. It quickly became apparent why she looked worried during games. "Would you pray that I would overcome my fear? I really like basketball, but I'm afraid I'm going to mess up. It worries me so much that it takes the fun out of playing. In fact I feel like a failure in everything." I led her in a brief prayer asking the Lord to bless her with the holy fear of God and thus break that unholy fear of failure. I watched her countenance change over the next few games. Her tense expression began to relax. She looked like she was having fun—and her game improved! She became much more aggressive in attempting shots and stealing the ball from her opponents. I cheered louder than ever. Those around me may have thought that I was just cheering for the team, but my excitement was over the goodness of God. Once again God was making sure that the greater fear broke the power of a lesser fear in the life of one He loved. Score another victory for the Father.

4 - Fear of Rejection

"Nevertheless many even of the rulers believed in Him, but because of the Pharisees they were not confessing Him, lest they should be put out of the synagogue." John 12:42

Peer pressure was at work in high places. Many Hebrew leaders saw, heard and believed in Jesus, but a paralyzing fear prevented them from acting in accordance with what they knew to be right. They were afraid the "in crowd", the Pharisees, would disapprove and expel them from the synagogue. They would have been surprised to know that the men they feared were also restrained by fear. *"When they [the Pharisees] sought to seize Him, they became afraid of the multitudes,..."* (Matthew 21:46). Peer pressure is built on fear. "Do it this way or they will reject you."

Though I did not realize it, the fear of people's rejection controlled me for years. In my role as a pastor I was expected to lead my congregation in spiritual matters. Often I prayed to God, asking for wisdom and insight so that I would know how to fulfill this leadership role in my church. Those who are familiar with prayer will not be surprised to know that God regularly gave me the guidance for which I asked.

Nevertheless, there was a dynamic at work in my

heart that complicated matters. Whenever the things I thought I was hearing from God seemed as though they would be acceptable to the congregation, I would eagerly receive God's counsel and boldly encourage the church to follow me. Sometimes, however, it seemed that God was leading in ways that I did not understand, or that I thought would be unpopular with leaders in the congregation or with my peers in my denomination. On such occasions I would simply quit listening to God. This was not an intentional action on my part. It was just that my fear of rejection by my congregation or by my fellow pastors raised such noisy tumult in my heart that it drowned out God's voice. I was listening to the wrong thing. Without realizing it, I allowed my desire for the approval of men to override my commitment to do as God directed. I was afraid to find out what would happen if people disagreed with me, or misunderstood my motives, or refused to cooperate with the plans I thought were from God.

There is a verse of Scripture that describes what was going on within me. *"Transgression speaks to the ungodly within his heart; There is no fear of God before his eyes"* (Psalm 36:1). Since I lacked the holy fear of the Lord, I had become subject to a restricting fear of rejection by people who were important to me. This led me into the sin of choosing to let man's pressure instead of God's voice determine my course of action. For me Sunday was incomplete if I did not stand at the exit after services and shake hands with the worshipers as they left for home. I was genuinely interested in them and wanted that personal touch in the midst of the busyness of life. But that was not the only reason I stationed myself where people would come face to face with me when they left church. I wanted their approval. I needed them to tell me that they liked my sermon or that God did something in their lives through my ministry. I craved affirmation. If the approval I looked for from the people was missing, I wrestled with a sense of failure. If they spoke favorably, it fed my craving but did not satisfy it. Within hours I would be thinking ahead to the next Sunday. Into my heart would creep the pressure of finding a way to gain their approval again the next time we worshiped. The cycle was relentless. Then came the day described in the first chapter of this book. While I was praying in the chapel God graciously encountered me and left holy fear in His wake. I found myself consumed with the desire to please Him. What others thought about my walk with Him became irrelevant. I still cared about my ability to lead the church God had called me to pastor, but that desire was no longer shaped by my fear of what the congregation thought of me. Rather it was driven by a hunger to see others experience His grace and love, and a desire to see our church glorify Him in the community around us. It was not that I battled my fear of man and overcame it. I was not aware of any battle at all. I had no need to struggle against this unholy fear because a newfound reverence for my awesome God had simply banished it from my heart.

The Sunday after He graciously taught my heart to fear, I stood again in the pulpit of my church. I was the same man, serving the same God, standing before the same people. But there was a significant difference. The pressure was off. Pleasing people no longer topped my agenda. That change made all the difference for me. For the first time I understood the Apostle Paul's words, *"I determined to know nothing among you except Jesus Christ, and Him crucified. And I was with you in weakness and in fear and in much trembling"* (1 Corinthians 2:2-3). That Sunday I was possessed by a fear and was weak and trembling. However, it wasn't those before whom I stood that engendered that fear. It was the One for whom I stood. For the first time in the history of that young suburban congregation they had a pastor who could stand in the pulpit and declare his understanding of God without shaping it to accommodate his fear of men.

You may ask, "Well, Brad, did the people follow you? Did the story have a happy ending?" I must tell you that everything I used to fear that people might do to me they have done. I have been misunderstood, rejected, slandered, abandoned and opposed by some. On the other hand, many others have appreciated, embraced, supported, instructed and enriched me. In the process I have learned something that has given me stability in times of affirmation and rejection. I have learned that I am not responsible for pleasing the congregations I serve. There will always be mixed reviews. There will always be some who reject me even though I'm right and there will be those who affirm me even when I'm dead wrong. I am learning to say with Paul, *"...it is a very small thing that I should be examined by you, or by any human court; in fact, I do not even examine myself. I am conscious of nothing against myself, yet I am not by this acquitted; but the one who examines me is the Lord"* (1 Corinthians 4:3-4).

Pleasing God versus Pleasing Men

One day a thought entered my mind that I think came from heaven. It seemed that God said, "It will be easier for you to please Me than for you to please your congregation." That truth liberated me from some upside-down thinking. I had been thinking that it would be impossible to please God. "After all," my subcon-

It really is easier to please God than men. scious reasoned, "He is so high and holy. Who can please Him?" So I set my sights lower. "I'll just try to please men." The good news for us reformed men pleasers is that it really is easier to please God than men. The reasons for this are found in the character of the One we wish to please.

- First, the Lord is holy, but men are sinful. Sin perverts our experience of pleasure. Even the best people are inconsistent in what pleases them. They sometimes delight in that which is unholy or detest what is true. This is not so with God. That which is good always pleases Him. That which is not good always displeases Him. He is consistent. I do not have to guess what will please Him.
- Second, the Lord is whole while men are fractured and divided. Thus what pleases some men will displease others. God is wholly integrated. *"Hear, O Israel! The LORD is our God, the LORD is one!"* (Deuteronomy 6:4). There is no confusion about pleasing God.
- Third, the Lord is unchanging, but men are unpredictable. A wife may please her husband by something she does one day only to discover that the action no longer pleases him another day. I do not

have to worry that God will change.
- Fourth, the Lord is Spirit, but men—even redeemed ones—struggle with the flesh. What pleases the highest prompting in a man's heart does not please his flesh. Because He is Spirit, God does not wrestle with carnal impulses in His nature. Like Jesus, I am to live my life before an audience of One. Jesus would not commit himself to men because he knew what was in their hearts (John 2:24-25). Instead he always committed himself to the Father and was ever pleasing to Him (Matthew 3:17).

So, next Sunday come to the church where I am preaching and after the service you might find me at the front door shaking hands. It will be all right if you do not compliment my sermon. You might even help me if we talk about something else. You see, I am trying not to place too much importance on the judgments of men. Too much of that noise could drown out the voice of my Master. After all, I want to hear Him clearly if He gives me an "Atta boy!" or an "Oh, no!"

5 - Fear of Death
"… free those who all their lives were held in slavery by their fear of death." Hebrews 2:15 NIV

Sheila may be the most courageous woman I know.

On Christmas day in 1989, she underwent transplant surgery in which she received a new heart and lungs. For transplant patients an ongoing fight against rejection rages in their bodies. The body identifies the new organs as foreign substances and attacks them to destroy them. The struggle has become how to keep Sheila's body from destroying the new organs that are sustaining her life.

Since before the surgery, Sheila has lived with the knowledge that death could come soon for her. Yet fear does not dominate her. On those occasions when the threat of organ rejection has jeopardized her life, she has honestly faced the situation and courageously maintained a healthy and positive stance for life. One of the keys to her ability to cope with this stress is that early in the process she discovered the power of the fear of the Lord. This morning, as I write this chapter, Sheila and her husband Rob are driving to Houston, Texas, for another round of treatments. "It's unpleasant," she told me, "and I do experience fear, but I have found that the fear of the Lord diffuses my fear of dying. He has given me a heart of praise."

Death is man's oldest enemy. The fear of death can cast a long shadow that robs us of the enjoyment life offers. When the nation of Israel was delivered from

400 years of slavery in Egypt, they gathered around Mount Sinai to worship God. The Lord's presence was made manifest in such awesome thunder, lightning and smoke that engulfed the mountain that the people *"... trembled with fear. They stayed at a distance and said to Moses, 'Speak to us yourself and we will listen. But do not have God speak to us or we will die'"* (Exodus 20:18-19 NIV). The Scripture is clear that the fear they experienced was not a holy reverence for God, but panic at the prospect of death. Their fear of death determined their reaction to the amazing happenings around them. Moses' response demonstrated a remarkable wisdom. *"Do not be afraid,"* he said. *"God has come to test you, so that the fear of God will be with you to keep you from sinning"* (See Exodus 20:20 NIV). Moses knew that two fears fought for dominance in the lives of the Israelites. One of the fears was healthy and one was not. He recognized that the people were being driven by the destructive fear of death. This fear led them to make an unwise decision to distance themselves from God. So he encouraged them not to let that unholy fear control them. He urged them instead to understand that God was demonstrating His presence in amazing fashion so that a healthy fear of the Lord would give them the courage to approach God and impel their lives toward genuine goodness. The fear of death is not easily overcome, but the fear of God is able to break the power

of this greatest of unholy fears.

It's Time to Face Your Fears

God delights in delivering us from the power of unholy, destructive fears. One of the ways He does this is by planting the holy fear of the Lord in our hearts. That greater fear breaks the power of lesser fears to dominate our lives. The possession of a healthy fear of the Lord does not insure that we will never experience a negative fear, but it does bring into our lives a wonderful resource by which we can respond with courage to all of life's circumstances. If you would like to join the many people who have discovered first hand that courage comes to those who fear God, may I suggest that you make the following prayer your own?

> *Dear Lord,*
> *The truth is I am afraid. I know that You are able to bring the healthy fear of God into my life in such a way as to bless me and to conquer the destructive fears within me. I humbly ask You now to plant reverent fear within my heart and teach me to grow in this grace. May You grant me the courage that comes with holy fear so that I may live life to the fullest and fulfill Your highest desires for me.*
> *In Jesus' Name, Amen.*
>
> "His mercy is upon generation after generation towards those who fear Him." Luke 1:50

Chapter Three

From God's Heart to Yours

"...I will inspire them to fear me..."
    Jeremiah 32:40 NIV

Would you like to see into the heart of God? Of course a direct gaze into the bright sunshine of His glory would be too much to bear. Just a glimpse will do. Indeed God has prepared a way for us to look into His heart. Waiting in the pages of Scripture are brilliant revelations for those who have eyes to see and striking chords for those who have ears to hear. One such passage is Deuteronomy 5:29. This verse takes us back to the day Jehovah established covenant with ancient Israel. The nation newly liberated from slavery in Egypt had gathered around Mount Sinai to worship their God. The mountain pulsated with the divine heartbeat while God spoke to Moses and the people waited below. Listen to His words. No. Do more than that. Listen for the heartbeat behind the words.

"Oh that they had such a heart in them, that they would fear Me, and keep all My commandments always, that it may be well with them and with their sons forever!"

There, did you hear it? The yearning of God! Can you feel the entrenched passion he openly shared with His prophet-friend Moses? It is the desire of His heart that we fear Him.

It is God's continual desire that holy fear be an appropriate part of the response of man to his Creator.

Lest you think that it was only for that particularly or those particular people, scan the pages of the Old and New Testaments and you will find over 150 explicit statements, commending to us the fear of the Lord. It has been and is God's continual desire that holy fear be an appropriate part of the response of man to his Creator.

That which has resided in the heart of God since His early dealings with man is individually planted in the heart of each person who enters into covenant with God. The fear of God is inextricably woven into the fabric of God's dealings with His people. Many years after the encounter on Mount Sinai, He again revealed His heart's desire on the day He made Jeremiah His voice. Describing the New Covenant to be established through Jesus Christ, God declared His intention. *"I will give them singleness of heart and action, so that they will always fear me for their own good and the good Of their children after them. I will make an everlasting covenant with them: ... and I will inspire them to fear me, so that they will never turn away from me"* (Jeremiah 32:39-40 NIV).

God is to be feared.
- **It is true in heaven.** Ascend to the highest heaven and find the familiar pulse in the eternal council of the heavenly hosts. *"For who in the skies above can compare with the LORD? Who is like the LORD among the heavenly beings? In the council of the holy ones God is greatly feared; he is more awesome than all who surround him"* (Psalm 89:6-7 NIV).
- **It is true for today.** When speaking to the New Testament church Peter said, *"Since you call on a Father who judges each man's work impartially, live your lives as strangers here in reverent fear"* (1 Peter 1:17 NIV).

- **It is true forever.** John saw an angel who proclaimed "the eternal gospel" that has no beginning or end. The first note sounded in this eternal gospel is "Fear God." *"Then I saw another angel flying in midair, and he had the eternal gospel to proclaim to those who live on the earth—to every nation, tribe, language and people. He said in a loud voice, 'Fear God and give him glory'"* (Revelation 14:6-7a NIV).

In days gone by, today, and forever God is to be feared. He has shown us His heart's desire. Once discovered, that desire becomes our duty. So how do we begin? What is this fear that is due His name?

What is the fear of the Lord?

The fear of the Lord is more than a concept to be conveyed from one mind to another. Strictly speaking it is evoked more than taught and awakened more than analyzed. It is highly reasonable, yet it goes farther than reason alone can take us. There are emotions that attend it, but it is so much more than a feeling. The Biblical descriptions of it focus on how it acts more than on what it is. The fear of the Lord is the awe filled awakening of the human heart to the undeniable call to approach the overwhelming majesty of our Creator God.

It is so much more than a feeling.

The five facets of holy fear

I believe there are at least five elements contained in the amazing fear that God says is the beginning of wisdom. Rudolf Otto, in his book, *The Idea of the Holy*, defined in detail the fear of the Lord. His thoughts have been helpful to me in developing my understanding of the nature of Biblical reverence. In the following examination of the five facets of holy fear, I have drawn upon Otto's work, adapting his thoughts to reflect my understanding and adding a Biblical example of each concept.

1. **The element of majesty.** Holy fear assaults us with the wonder of God's exalted station. His loftiness is unattainable, His might is unquestionable and His authority is undeniable. Recognition of His majesty causes us to tremble at the invitation to approach God. We know that it would be utter foolishness to enter His Presence uninvited, but no less foolish to neglect to enter when called. One example of this aspect of the fear of the Lord can be seen on the day that God gave the Ten Commandments. *"And all the people perceived the thunder and the lightning flashes and the sound of the trumpet and the mountain smoking; and when the people saw it, they trembled and stood at a distance"* (Exodus 20:18). The

mountain smoked and the ground shook. God's power was displayed in such a fashion that everyone present knew that it was a deadly serious thing to witness the majesty of God. No one suggested, "Let's get closer so we can see the show." Neither did anyone dare to turn his back on the One who spoke from the throne. So they "stood at a distance." They stood because one should not run from majesty. They maintained their distance because one should not approach majesty uninvited.

2. **The element of humility.** In the fear of God there is a keen creature consciousness, the emotion of a created being overwhelmed by its own littleness in contrast to that which is supreme above all creatures. In the presence of the One who has created us, overblown self importance is banished by the stark and frightening realization of how much greater He is, as Creator, than we are as the ones He created. When the prophet Isaiah experienced holy fear, he saw the Lord in a new light. He also saw himself in an entirely new light.

"In the year of King Uzziah's death, I saw the Lord sitting on a throne, lofty and exalted, with the train of His robe filling the temple. Seraphim stood above Him, each having six wings; with two he covered his face, and with two he

covered his feet, and with two he flew. And one called out to another and said, 'Holy, Holy, Holy, is the LORD of hosts, the whole earth is full of His glory.' And the foundations of the thresholds trembled at the voice of Him who called out, while the temple was filling with smoke. Then I said, 'Woe is me, for I am ruined! Because I am a man of unclean lips, And I live among a people of unclean lips; For my eyes have seen the King, the LORD of hosts'" (Isaiah 6:1-5).

The fear of God imparts a humility that makes it impossible to strut casually into His presence. Sanctimonious pride cannot compete for even a corner of our hearts when godly fear takes hold. Genuine fear of God always produces the clear recognition of our unworthiness before Him.

3. **The element of mystery.** Holy fear brings us to the realization that God transcends the usual, the intelligible, and the familiar. God is fully reasonable, but goes far beyond where reason alone can take anyone. He is too big to embrace and too amazing to comprehend. God dwells beyond the narrow capacity of language or thought, and thus fills the mind with blank wonder and astonishment. During the course of what was probably a typical day of ministry for Jesus, he forgave a man's sins and then healed his paralyzed body. The response

of those who witnessed this miracle was not uncommon among those who crossed Christ's path. *"And they were all seized with astonishment and began glorifying God; and they were filled with fear, saying, 'We have seen remarkable things today'"* (Luke 5:26). The Lord's activity was of such magnitude that those who saw what He did could not process it mentally. The sight of God at work so overloaded their reasoning capacity that their minds went blank with astonishment. Blank wonder is one aspect of holy fear.

4. The element of awe. This concept is from the Hebrew word *hiqdish* (to hallow), which means to mark off by a feeling of peculiar dread. It is the word that Jesus used when he taught his disciples to pray. *"And He said to them, 'When you pray, say: Father, hallowed be Thy name'"* (Luke 11:2). It is as though a line were drawn distinguishing God from all that is unlike Him. The element of awe refuses to blur the line that restrains us from treating the holy as profane or the profane as holy. Awe makes it unthinkable to attempt to bring His holiness across the line into the realm of the common or profane. For example, people whose hearts are gripped with awe would never use God's name as an expletive to express disgust or frustration. That would be crossing the line. Nor would God-fearing people cross the line in the other direction by attempting to bring anything unholy with them when they answer the call to enter His Presence. Awe reminds us to search our hearts. *"Who may ascend into the hill of the LORD? And who may stand in His holy place? He who has clean hands and a pure heart"* (Psalms 24:3-4a). On the day that Jesus was crucified, two criminals were executed on either side of Him. Early in the gruesome ordeal Matthew tells of the verbal abuse thrown at Jesus. He makes it clear that *"... the robbers also who had been crucified with Him were casting the same insult at Him"* (Matthew 27:44). However, during the hours that the three of them endured together the anguish of Roman crosses, a change took place in one of the thieves. He no longer hurled abuse at Jesus. In fact he became offended at his companion, who continued to taunt Christ. We know that awe had gripped his heart because of the nature of the rebuke he delivered to his cohort in crime. *"Do you not even fear God?"* (Luke 23:40). Awe caused him to recoil at the thought of allowing profane speech to be addressed to the holy One beside him. Awe acknowledges the "set-apart-ness" of God and finds it unthinkable to treat the Lord as less than holy.

5. **The element of attraction.** Godly-fear carries with it the impulse born of fascination which

causes us to turn to Him and remain fixed upon, Him even as we tremble before Him. As surely as a magnet exerts a pull upon metal filings, holy fear draws our focus to the Lord and rivets our attention upon Him. This pull is the heart's desire for nearness to Him that compels us to cry out, "This is what I was created for."

Everywhere Jesus went he left a wake of holy fear. Surprisingly, this fear caused people to gather around Him in utter fascination. Rather than running in fear, they were drawn by holy fear to continue near Him. The Gospel of Mark illustrates this clearly, *"And they were on the road, going up to Jerusalem, and Jesus was walking on ahead of them; and they were amazed, and those who followed were fearful"* (Mark 10:32). Here we find a picture of Jesus walking along a road with His twelve disciples. Others within earshot, follow along because of their fascination with Christ. According to Mark these onlookers simultaneously experienced fear and attraction. The attraction drew them to Him, and kept them from turning away in spite of the racing rhythm of their hearts. Similarly, today's believers who possess a holy fear of God are

> **Believers who possess a holy fear of God are drawn to focus on and follow the Lord.**

drawn to focus on and follow the Lord.

Make His pulse your passion.

I hope you have a sense of the yearning in God's heart for His people to fear Him. That divine desire is revealed repeatedly in Scripture, but in order for the fear of the Lord to become the blessing God intended, it must make the journey from God's heart to your heart. His pulse must become your passion. I invite you to join me in the exciting adventure that comes to those who pray, "Lord, teach me to fear You." He is eager to show you the way.

Part 2
Finding Your Way

*How Precious did that Grace Appear
the Hour I First Believed.*

Chapter Four

The One Who Showed the Way

"He will delight in the fear of the Lord." Isaiah 11:3

When I began to study what the Scriptures teach concerning the fear of the Lord, I was not sure I wanted to experience fear in my relationship with Him. I wondered how healthy it would be to actually cultivate fear of the Lord. I worried about the negative impact it might have on my intimacy with Him and my love for Him. Would I still experience peace or comfort? Could fear push me into legalism? Would it rob me of joy? I knew the conflict within me would have to be resolved and I determined to let Jesus cast the deciding ballot. I set out to study every Biblical passage in which Jesus shed light on the fear of the Lord. My thinking was, "If I can understand how Jesus stood on the issue, then I'll know how I should stand on it. If He embraced the fear of the Lord, then I'm going to embrace it, too. If I can't find it in Jesus, I don't want anything to do with it." It was my intent to find out what Jesus thought and taught, and then line up with Him.

What I discovered surprised me and released me to receive one of the most amazing expressions of grace I have known. After extensive study of the Word of God, I came to an unshakable conclusion. It was this. Nowhere can you see the fear of God so vividly personified as in the life of Jesus Christ. In fact Scripture reveals Jesus to be the perfect embodiment of the holy fear of the Lord. Years before the birth of Jesus in Bethlehem, Isaiah described the Messiah in this way: *"The Spirit of the LORD will rest on him— the Spirit of wisdom and of understanding, the Spirit of counsel and of power, the Spirit of knowledge and of the fear of the LORD—and he will delight in the fear of the LORD."* Isaiah 11:2-3 NIV

The prophet predicted that the Spirit of the Lord would rest (or remain) on Jesus. Isaiah then described the Spirit as, among other things, *"the Spirit...of the fear of the Lord."* The Holy Spirit, who expressed the very life of God in Jesus, had as part of His essence the fear of the Lord. Remarkably, the fear of the Lord would be a delight to the Messiah.

How was this aspect of the essential nature of the Christ expressed? For the answer we turn to the New Testament narratives of the life of Christ, where we see Him evoke this holy fear by His actions, encourage it through His teaching, and embrace it in His own walk with the Father.

1 - Jesus produced the fear of the Lord by His presence.

Jesus regularly broke the power of destructive fears in the lives of people but He never sought to remove the fear of God from anyone's heart. In fact, as Jesus moved through this world He left in His wake a response of holy fear. It was the consistent reaction of people stunned by the presence and activity of the Son of God made flesh.

In whom did Jesus produce holy fear?

- <u>In those who followed Him</u> (Mark 4:35-41).

The disciples knew they were in trouble. As veteran fishermen they had seen storms arise quickly before.

It looked as though this would be their last battle with the sea. The boat was going down and fear took over. In contrast to the turmoil in their hearts, Jesus slept peacefully in the back of the boat. So they rushed to him. *"Teacher, do You not care that we are perishing?"* He rose to his feet and did what He so often does for frightened men and women. He took away their reason to fear. *"Hush, be still,"* he said. Immediately the winds above vanished while the sea's surface became perfectly still.

Since death was no longer a threat, we would expect the disciples to have regained their composure at this point. Instead their fear increased. *"And they became very much afraid."* It wasn't fear of death that held them now. It was the fear of God. No longer was the fate of the boat their concern. Rather their focus had become the One who was with them in the boat. *"Who then is this, that even the wind and the sea obey Him?"*

- In those who opposed Him (Mark 1:21-28).

It was the Sabbath and Jesus was teaching in the synagogue. If those in attendance were expecting a typical study of the scripture, they were in for a surprise. As happened repeatedly during his ministry, the presence of Jesus provoked a commotion in the spirit world. *"Just then a man in their synagogue who was possessed by an evil spirit cried out, 'What do you want with us, Jesus of Nazareth? Have you come to destroy us? I know who you are—the Holy One of God!'"* (Mark 1:24 NIV). Satan's strategy of maintaining an influence in the synagogue depended upon secrecy, but Christ's presence flushed the evil spirit out of hiding. Another New Testament passage pictures the fearful response to Jesus that is common within the kingdom of darkness: *"the devils also believe, and tremble."* (See James 2:19 KJV) Fear of God compelled the demonic enemies of Christ to wave the white flag of surrender and plead for mercy.

• <u>In those who observed His ministry</u> (Mark 5:15 NIV).

"When they came to Jesus, they saw the man who had been possessed by the legion of demons, sitting there, dressed and in his right mind; and they were afraid." The villagers knew they were in the presence of Power and they were unnerved. For years the entire town had tried to deal with the graveyard man but they were no match for his violence or strength. Unable to subdue him, they had finally surrendered the cemetery to him. There was nothing left but to warn the children to stay close to home and live with the uneasy knowledge of his nearness. Or so they thought...

Then Jesus came. What really frightened the townspeople was that Jesus possessed more than the power to conquer. He had the power to transform. Without breaking a sweat he had remade a man. No wonder they were afraid.

- <u>In those who received His touch</u> (Mark 5:33-34 NIV).

She had fearlessly forced the issue. Refusing to let the crowd remain an obstacle to reaching Him, the woman elbowed her way into a position to intersect His course. She had to be patient and quick, but finally her opportunity came. The teacher walked within arm's length. She thrust out her hand, barely touching the edge of His cloak, but it was enough. Heat moved through her, flowing from hand to heart. Not until then did she become afraid. Trembling took her body as the realization broke upon her. She had been healed yes, but that had become almost unimportant. What mattered now was that she had been touched. It was more than physical. Something in that touch changed everything.

That's when He stopped and called for her. Fear drew her to Him. It was not a fear of having overstepped her bounds with a presumptuous grab for His garment. It was not a fear of what He would now do to her or what others would think. It was not a fear that made her want to flee. It was greater than any of those. She knew that the only thing that mattered was that she be at His feet, opening her heart, worshiping her Maker. *"Then the woman, knowing what had happened to her, came and fell at his feet and, trembling with fear, told him the whole truth. He said to her, 'Daughter, your faith has healed you. Go in peace and be freed from your suffering.'"*

What was it about Him that produced fear?

His birth. *"And there were shepherds living out in the fields nearby, keeping watch over their flocks at night. An angel of the Lord appeared to them, and the glory of the Lord shone around them, and they were terrified."* (Luke 2:8-9 NIV)

His power. *"Then he went up and touched the coffin, and those carrying it stood still. He said, 'Young man, I say to you, get up!' The dead man sat up and began to talk, and Jesus gave him back to his mother. They were all filled with awe and praised God."* (Luke 7:14-16a NIV)

His glory. *"Jesus took Peter, James and John with him and led them up a high mountain, where they were all alone. There he was transfigured before them. His clothes became dazzling white, whiter than anyone in the world could bleach them Peter said to Jesus, 'Rabbi, it is good for us to be here. Let us put up three shelters—one for you, one for Moses and one for Elijah.' (He did not know what to say, they were so fright-*

ened.)" (Mark 9:2-6 NIV)

His teaching. *"He said to them, 'The Son of Man is going to be betrayed into the hands of men. They will kill him, and after three days he will rise." But they did not understand what he meant and were afraid to ask him about it."* (Mark 9:31-32 NIV)

His daily walk. *"They were on their way up to Jerusalem, with Jesus leading the way, and the disciples were astonished, while those who followed were afraid."* (Mark 10:32a NIV)

His death. *"One of the criminals who hung there hurled insults at him: 'Aren't you the Christ? Save yourself and us!' But the other criminal rebuked him, 'Don't you fear God... ?'"* (Luke 23:39-40 NIV)

His resurrection. *"So the women hurried away from the tomb, afraid yet filled with joy, and ran to tell his disciples."* (Matthew 28:8 NIV)

2 - Jesus encouraged the fear of the Lord in His teaching.

He taught us whom to fear.

Following Jesus has always been dangerous. Opposition to Christ and Christians has taken violent form in every generation. The Lord knew that even the boldest of believers would wrestle with the fear that persecution provokes. In this context came the teaching of Christ about the proper object of our fear. His words hold a special relevance to any believer who has to stand against the tide of anger that can follow obedience to the One this world crucified. *"I tell you, my friends, do not be afraid of those who kill the body and after that can do no more. But I will show you whom you should fear: Fear him who, after the killing of the body, has power to throw you into hell. Yes, I tell you, fear him"* (Luke 12:4-5 NIV). Only God can throw us into hell. No man has that power. Not even the devil can sentence us to hell. Only the Father in heaven has the authority to determine a soul's eternal destiny. So, Jesus taught not that we should fear God will send us to hell, but that we should fear Him as the One who possesses that kind of authority.

He taught us how to pray.

A second example of Christ's explicit teaching on the subject of the fear of the Lord is found in his instructions on how to pray. The first petition Jesus taught us to offer in His model prayer for believers (Luke 11:2-4) is the request that the name of the Father in heaven would be "hallowed." The Hebrew word means to set apart with a peculiar feeling of dread. It is no accident that this petition is placed first among the things Jesus taught us to pray. Until there is a posture of reverence in the heart of man for his Creator, he is in no position to engage in the business of the kingdom (v. 2), request the daily provision of his needs (v. 3), give and receive forgiveness (v. 4), or wrestle with temptation (v. 4). Of the things for which Christ taught us to pray, reverent fear tops the list.

3 - Jesus embraced the fear of the Lord in His relationship with the Father.

There are some mysteries that are unfathomable. This story is told about the great reformer Martin Luther. One morning on the way to his study he gave instructions that he was not to be disturbed. He had determined that he would spend the entire day meditating on the words Jesus spoke from the cross, "My God, my God, why hast Thou forsaken me?" Before long, it is said, he emerged from his contemplation and was heard to murmur, "God forsaken of God? Who can understand that?"

Perhaps when I say to you that Jesus feared His heavenly Father, you will have a similar response. "God fearing God? Who can understand that?" But the revelation of Scripture is clear. Jesus not only taught the fear of the Lord. He experienced it!

Nowhere can we see this more clearly than when we examine the prayer life of the Lord. There are numerous places in the Gospels in which the prayers of Jesus are recorded. He had unquestioned power in prayer. His disciples observed this and asked Him to teach them how to pray. There is one Bible passage that opens for us a mystery. In it we find the reason Jesus had such power in prayer. *"Who in the days of his flesh, when he had offered up prayers and supplications with strong crying and tears unto him that was able to save him from death, and was heard in that he feared"* (Hebrews 5:7 KJV).

Following Christ

Our Lord Jesus has precisely defined for us the place that genuine, reverent fear is to take in our relationship with God. He did more than speak of it. He incarnated the truth of it in his teaching, ministry actions and walk with the Father. Because I see this grace in his life, I am emboldened to receive it into my own life. For the one who follows Christ will, like Him, "delight in the fear of the Lord."

Chapter Five

How We Lost Our Way

"...And the dread of Me is not in you..." Jeremiah 2:19

Often God has had to confront His people because they have fallen into a state of spiritual emptiness and general failure. In His loving confrontation of us lies our best hope for renewal. When God sent Jeremiah to challenge Israel, He diagnosed their malady with the declaration, *"And the dread of Me is not in you."* They had lost their fear of God!

Survey the church in America today and the words of Jeremiah seem to ring with relevance. *"And the dread of Me is not in you."* For the most part the Biblical teach-

Some are offended at the idea that God is to be feared. ings on the fear of God have been overlooked, ignored, and even rejected by the modem church. It is a major theme of Scripture, yet few are aware of the importance of this doctrine. In fact, it has been my experience that some are offended at the idea that God is to be feared.

Nevertheless, God is calling His church to a rediscovery of the biblical imperative. He is restoring in His people the holy fear of the Lord, which is a *"fountain of life"* (Proverbs 14:27). In finding our way back to a balanced biblical position it would be helpful to examine the question of how we lost our way. Why has the plain teaching of Scripture on the fear of the Lord been neglected or discarded by so many in the Christian community? Let me suggest eight possible answers.

1 - Because of the assumption that fearing God means fleeing from Him, when in fact the opposite is true.

The healthy fear of the Lord is like glue in that it bonds our hearts to God. It is not a wedge that drives us from Him. Moses understood this when he told the people that *"God has come in order to test you, and in order that the fear of Him may remain with you, so that you may not sin"* (Exodus 20:20). God's plan was to oppose sin, which separates us from God, by instilling a healthy fear of Him, which bonds us to Him. A child's disobedience may make her want to run away from her parents, but a healthy fear of them will conquer her urge to flee and steady her resolve to approach them even if she knows discipline awaits her. Similarly, the fear of the Lord will overcome the fear of His discipline in our lives. Through reverence we find the steadiness to stay in touch with our Maker even when we know He is going to correct us in love. Jeremiah also understood the drawing power of holy fear when he presented the promise of God concerning His new covenant with man. *"I will put the fear of Me in their hearts so that they will not turn away from Me"* (Jeremiah 32:40). An incident in the life of American revivalist Charles G. Finney illustrates the way in which holy fear draws us to God. Finney reported in his memoirs that he had a vision in 1826. In the vision Christ drew so near to him while he was praying that Finney's whole body trembled from head to foot. This was an intense experience of awe and humility before God. In Finney's words, "Instead of feeling like fleeing, I seemed drawn nearer and nearer to God, seemed to draw nearer and nearer to that Presence that filled me with such unutterable awe and trembling."[1]

2 - Because of the failure to distinguish between healthy fear and unhealthy fears.

> God takes delight in setting us free from such unhealthy fears.

Some may assume that all fear is negative, destructive of the human spirit, and should be conquered rather than cultivated. It is true that unhealthy fears abound, along with counterfeits of the proper fear of the Lord. These destructive fears enslave men and women, robbing them of their capacity to move forward in life. God takes delight in setting us free from such unhealthy fears. It is also true that when God created us with a capacity to fear, He did not make a mistake. Healthy fear is vital for healthy living.

Suppose I were walking along a railroad track and heard the approach of a train from behind me. The vibrations along the rails and the shrill whistle bearing down on me would cause a panic throughout my body. That fear would scream at me to give way to the train. What if I overcame that fear and maintained my place? Obviously such foolish courage would get me killed. Proper fear will make sure I jump the tracks and live to tell about it. That is a fear I would rather not lose.

I had been teaching on the fear of the Lord for a couple of months when a member of the congregation came to me with a question. "Pastor, won't talking about fearing God have a negative psychological effect on our children?" As we talked a steady stream of squealing, happy children pranced around us. I said, "See for yourself. They have heard all that I have said about fearing God and it hasn't diminished their joy one bit." Why are we quick to teach our children a healthy fear of fire and never assume that such teaching will constitute mental abuse. We teach them a healthy fear of traffic, but don't worry about damaging them psychologically. We know that healthy fear will save their lives. So, we should not hesitate to teach them the healthy fear of God.

Fear of God is good for us. In fact when that fear is absent from our lives, we are by default gripped with unhealthy fears. Our capacity to fear is still operative even though we have lost the proper object for our fear. We still fear, only now we fear the wrong things. It is only when we cultivate the healthy fear of God that we are enabled to conquer those unhealthy fears against which we rightly struggle.

3 - Because some have redefined the Scriptures to explain the fear of God in terms of respect only.

There are those who say, "I fear God, but I'm not afraid of Him." By this they mean that they have respect for God, but dread and terror have no place in their relationship with the Almighty. There was a time when I would have applauded that sentiment, but no more. I find it difficult to imagine Isaiah drawing such a distinction in the temple when he said, *"'Woe to me!' I cried, 'I am ruined! For... my eyes have seen the King, the LORD Almighty'"* (Isaiah 6:5 NIV). Respect for God is certainly a major aspect of the fear of the Lord. However, honesty in handling the language God has chosen to describe the fear He requires leads us to conclude that there is more to this quality than respect alone. Scripture speaks of Jehovah being *"the fear of Isaac"* (Genesis 31:42) and of Paul *"knowing the terror of the Lord"* (2 Corinthians 7:1). Any understanding of the fear of the Lord that fails to encompass these aspects is certainly inadequate.

4 - The fear of the Lord involves humility and the prevailing spirit of our age has called upon us to exalt ourselves, not humble ourselves.

The fear of the Lord and humility go hand in hand. *"To this day they have not humbled themselves or shown reverence,..."* (Jeremiah 44:10 NIV). I must humble myself before I can show reverence, and humility is not a popular subject. Everywhere we are urged to give priority to how we can esteem ourselves. Proper self-esteem is needed, but we lose our bearings when self-esteem becomes the focus. What we really need is God esteem. We need to esteem God first and foremost and we need to be esteemed by God. Isaiah 66:2 tells us whom God esteems. *"This is the one I esteem: he who is humble and contrite in spirit, and trembles at my word"* (NIV). According to this verse the three qualities that we should seek to develop if we are interested in God's esteem are (1) humility, (2) contrition, and (3) reverent fear in regard to God's word.

Our age suspects that an experience of the fear of God will demean us when in fact it is precisely that experience which holds the key to our being clothed with the glory that our loving Creator has reserved for the crown of His creation. *"The fear of the LORD teaches a man wisdom, and humility comes before honor"* (Proverbs 15:33 NIV).

5 - Because the doctrine of the fear of God is sometimes confused with "fire and brimstone preaching."

Some misguided preachers have thought it was their

His holy fear is full of enriching grace. job to instill the fear of God in their hearers through their pulpit thunderings. This may produce a form of fear, but it is a counterfeit to the holy fear that binds our hearts to the Lord. Producing the fear of God is God's work, not man's. When men try to manipulate through fear, they demean people and distort God's character. There are a host of phobias foisted on people in the name of religion, but when God plants His holy fear in our hearts as part of His covenant with us, the experience is full of enriching grace.

When it comes to preaching, some like it hot and some don't. Whatever our preference we make a grave error when we equate an eternal truth of God, such as, man's duty to fear Him with a style of proclamation, especially if our dislike for the style causes us to dismiss the truth.

6 - Because we have substituted religious traditions for genuine reverence.

Alan was a Jewish convert to Christ. He had thick curly red hair, wore a yarmulke while in church and sat on the second row of the center section. One Sunday he made a move that took many of us by surprise. As soon as the singing began he lifted a hand high in the air as an expression of praise to God. It stayed stuck in the air throughout the singing portion of the service. At that time raising hands in our church was an unfamiliar practice. So it was no surprise that the chairman of the deacons came to me later and asked, "What are we going to do about Alan? We can't let him ruin our worship." Alan thought that what he was doing was an expression of reverence. The deacon considered it irreverent because it broke tradition. *"... their reverence for Me consists of tradition learned by rote"* (Isaiah 29:13). The Lord was not paying His people a compliment. They were substituting religious tradition for genuine reverence. It still happens today. Churches develop traditions including rituals of worship. These rituals may be written or unwritten, acknowledged formally or assumed informally. When I visited Israel I was expected to cover my head when entering a Jewish place of worship. When traveling in Oklahoma I had better take my hat off in church or I'll create a stir of indignation. In one fellowship reverence for God is defined as silent, somber reflection, while in another congregation just down the street, it is felt that you have not worshiped God unless you have offered Him boisterous expressions of love. Each group defines acceptable and unacceptable behaviors. Compliance with rules governing such things as dress codes, eating, drinking, or talking in church is sometimes equated with reverence. Nonconformity is viewed as irreverence toward God.

Genuine reverence is much more than conformity to tradition. The fact that we go to church and repeat the actions performed there each Sunday is no guarantee that we have worshiped. We make a serious mistake whenever we focus on traditions learned by repetition instead of the awesome experience of intimacy with the Creator. Worship is a matter of the heart, not of ritual.

7 - Because some have taught that the God of the New Testament is different from the God of the Old Testament.

Perhaps you have heard it said that the God of the Old Testament was a God of fear and justice, but that the God of the New Testament is a God of love and mercy. If this thinking were true, we could understand how some would conclude that fearing God is a primitive response from which modern man has graduated. We could also understand the claim that love has supplanted fear as the primary means of relating to God. But the fact is that God hasn't changed nor has the value of reverent fear changed.

God did not evolve over time into a "nicer" God.

He did not have a mid-life crisis between the Old and New Testaments and emerge with a new personality. The Shema, which is found in Deuteronomy 6:4, is declared at the beginning of synagogue services to this day. *"Hear, O Israel! the LORD is our God, the LORD is one!"* God is one not only in number but also in nature. He doesn't change. His character is constant. His qualities are immutable. Both the Old and New Testaments reveal God to be a God of love, mercy and compassion. Both also reveal God to be a God of fear, justice, holiness and power. The revelation of God is consistent throughout the Bible. Progressive understanding of God's character is something man may experience but progressive development of character is not something that God undergoes. He is today exactly what He was in the beginning and what He will be throughout eternity. The proper response of man to God is based on His divine character. Since His character has not changed, the way man should respond to Him today is identical to the way he was to respond to Him centuries ago. Man is still to love, obey and trust God. The fear of the Lord is still—and will continue to be—an appropriately necessary aspect of our relationship with the Almighty.

8 - Because of the mistaken idea that fearing God is incompatible with loving God.

Her friendly smile was transformed into a grandmotherly rebuke when she saw what I was reading. We were in the surgical waiting room of a hospital. I was waiting to learn the outcome of a friend's operation. She was a hospital volunteer. While bringing her warm cheer to the friends and families of patients, she spotted me with my book. "What are you reading?" she asked sweetly. I held it up for her to see. It was a copy of The Fear of God by John Bunyan, a 17th century doctrinal work by the author of The Pilgrim's Progress.

"The Fear of God? Oh my, God doesn't want you to be afraid of Him," she almost scolded.

"But..." I started to reply.

She would have none of it. Closing the conversation abruptly she said, "My God loves you and He wants you to love Him."

Those who love God will fear Him and those who have a healthy fear of God will love Him.

Is there a place for both fear and love in our relationship to God? Many find it difficult to reconcile the Biblical instruction to fear God with the teaching of Christ to love the Lord. This is understandable. Yet Jesus had no such difficulty. He taught us to do both. He taught us to love God: *"And He said to him, 'You shall love the Lord your God with all your heart, and with all your soul, and with all your mind.' This is the great commandment"* (Matthew 22:37-38). He taught us to fear God: *"I will show you whom you should fear: Fear him who, after the killing of the body, has power to throw you into hell. Yes, I tell you, fear him"* (Luke 12:5 NIV).

Paradoxical as it sounds, those who love God will fear Him and those who have a healthy fear of God will love Him. Then why do many people find it difficult to accept that the fear of God is compatible with loving God? I have frequently encountered two reasons for this struggle.

Doesn't perfect love cast out fear?

There is a question that has surfaced repeatedly in my conversations with people about the fear of God. It is this, "I thought the Bible said perfect love casts out all fear. So shouldn't my love for God remove any fear of Him?" That is a legitimate question and deserves a careful answer. The Bible passage in question is found in The First Letter of John.

"And we have come to know and have believed the love which God has for us. God is love, and the one who abides in love abides in God, and God abides in him. By this, love is perfected with us, that we may have confidence in the day of judgment, because as He is, so also are we in this world. There is no fear in love; but perfect love casts out fear, because fear involves punishment,

and the one who fears is not perfected in love." 1 John 4:16-18

1 John 4:16-18 does not say perfect love casts out all fear.

I should point out that verse 18 is often misquoted. It does not say perfect love casts out all fear. The word all is not present in the verse. John teaches us in these verses that our love relationship with the Father in heaven will dispel a specific fear which has plagued many people. What fear is being talked about in these verses? It is the fear we might feel when contemplating the final judgment of the human race by God. Uncertainty about our relationship with God would rightly provoke a fearful anticipation of what will happen to us when we stand before the Righteous Judge of all mankind. This is fear of judgment, rather than the holy fear of the Lord. John makes the point that those who abide in a love relationship with Christ need not suffer anxiety about judgment day. Rather their love for God imparts confidence, casting out the fear of punishment. All genuine believers can and should overcome the fear of what will happen to them when they stand before the judgment seat of heaven.

Nonetheless, John is not teaching that believers will feel no awe or reverence for Almighty God on the Day of Judgment. It is inconceivable that anyone could stand before Him and not be overwhelmed by the majesty of God, trembling at His greatness, gripped by reverence, riveted by the knowledge that His slightest desire demands our instant and total obedience.

More than an emotion

The second reason many people struggle to reconcile fearing God and loving Him is because of the conflicting emotions attendant to fear and love. We all know that love and fear feel differently. The feeings associated with fear may include a sharp alertness, disturbing discomfort, or peculiar sense of dread. In contrast the feelings that accompany love include delightful peace, soothing comfort and joy.

The emotions we feel.

Love for God	Fear of God
delight	dread
peace	terror
soothing comfort	discomfort
happiness	seriousness
relaxed enjoyment	alert readiness
exhilaration	astonishment

The essence of love for God and fear of God are not found in the fleeting feelings that accompany them.

We make a mistake when we define either love for God or fear of God by the changing emotions that often accompany them. Love is more than a feeling. Anyone who has been married longer than three days knows that. Feelings come and go, but love is a steady commitment. Love acts faithfully whatever it feels at the moment. Therefore, it is no surprise that when the Bible describes love for God, the focus is on what love does, not how love feels. The same is true for the fear of the Lord. It is much more than a feeling. It, too, is a steady commitment whose essence is discovered in what it does, not in how it feels. A comparison of the

How does it act?

Love for God	and	Fear of God
It Obeys 1 John 5:3		**It Obeys** Deuteronomy 5:29
It Abides 1 John 4:16		**It Abides** Jeremiah 32:40
It Hates evil Psalm 97:10		**It Hates evil** Proverbs 8:13
It Worships Isaiah 56:6-7		**It Worships** 2 Kings 17:36

The emotions attending the fear of God and love for God differ, but the essence (actions) of both are identical.

Biblical definitions of love for God and fear of God reveals an amazing truth. Both act in the same way!

When fear of God and love for God are united in the hearts of believers, those believers stand firmly in a doubly binding union of commitment with the Father regardless of what emotions they feel. The cord of love and the cord of reverence combine to lash their hearts to God in an intimacy that remains constant regardless of the emotions of any given moment.

Finding your way back

Even though the church has strayed from the truth that we are to fear God, there is hope. God knows we have lost our way in this matter and is moving to restore this precious grace to his people. There is a growing hunger among believers to understand God's desire for reverence and to walk in the holy fear of the Lord

---

[1] Wesley Duewel, Revival Fire (Grand Rapids: Zondervan Publishing House, 1995), P. 104

Chapter Six

Unlocking Heaven's Treasure

He will be the sure foundation for your times, a rich store of salvation and wisdom and knowledge; The fear of the LORD is the key to this treasure. Isaiah 33:6 (**NIV**)

Numerous blessings accompany intimacy with God. Repeatedly the Lord has expressed His desire to bestow rich gifts upon His people. It is as though a magnificent storehouse of treasure has been placed before us, filled with salvation, wisdom, strength, peace, joy, assurance, hope and more. Yet few find the way into the storehouse. Why don't more of us enjoy the rich array of wealth prepared for us? Isaiah tells us that there is a key that can unlock heaven for us and, just as important, unlock our hearts to heavenly delights. Such a key would be well worth finding and using. "The fear of the Lord is the key to this treasure." When we utilize this key we uncover what many have sought—the wisdom of the ages.

The Beginning of Wisdom

"There is a mine for silver and a place where gold is refined. But where can wisdom be found? The deep says, 'It is not in me'; the sea says, 'It is not with me'. Where then does wisdom come from? It is hidden from the eyes of every living thing, concealed even from the birds of the air. Destruction and Death say, 'Only a rumor of it has reached our ears.' God understands the way to it and he alone knows where it dwells. And he said to man, 'The fear of the Lord—that is wisdom.'" (Excerpted from the 28th chapter of Job)

When the world thinks of wise men, King Solomon usually tops the list. As a young man Solomon ascended to the throne of Israel. One night the Lord came to him and said, *"Ask for whatever you want me to give you"* (1 Kings 3:5 NIV).

What a remarkable opportunity! He could ask for anything and it would be his. Should he choose wealth? Many would have done so. Long life? That has been the pursuit of millions. Power to put down those who opposed his plans and purposes? Many have longed for that! Instead he chose something of greater value than any of these. He chose wisdom. And he never regretted the choice. In fact, later in life he concluded, *"For wisdom is better than jewels; and all desirable things can not compare with her"* (Proverbs 8:11).

Not only did Solomon possess wisdom, but he shared it with the world. Much of what he taught was compiled in the section of the Bible known as wisdom literature, to which he contributed the books of Proverbs, Ecclesiastes and The Song of Solomon. The pursuit of wisdom is a major theme of his writing and a worthy goal for us. So where do we start the search for wisdom?

The Bible often contrasts man's version of wisdom with God's version. The Apostle Paul wrote, *"The world through its wisdom did not come to know God."* He even declared, *"For the wisdom of this world is foolishness before God"* (1 Corinthians 1:21, 3:19a). We should understand that when Solomon taught *"the fear of the LORD is the beginning of wisdom"* (Proverbs 9:10), he was speaking of God's version of wisdom. Godly wisdom derives out of and is intimately tied to the fear of the Lord. Scripture unfolds this truth in three specific teachings.

1 - The fear of the Lord is the starting point of wisdom.

To say that the fear of the Lord is the beginning of wisdom means that fearing God is the place to start if we desire to know the wisdom of God. It is the key that unlocks the door. *"He [the Lord] will be the sure foundation for your times, a rich store of salvation and wisdom and knowledge; the fear of the LORD is the key to this treasure"* (Isaiah 33:6 NIV).

To seek wisdom while bypassing the fear of the Lord is a fruitless endeavor. If we want to enter a room we must walk through the door. If we desire to enter into the wisdom of God we must experience the fear of God because it is the door that provides access. In a similar vein the starting point for the Christian life is to enter into a personal relationship with Jesus Christ. He described himself as the door (John 10:9). We can observe Christianity without walking through that door, but we cannot be Christian until we pass through the portal of personal relationship with Christ. In wisdom, as in Christianity, we must begin at the starting point.

> To seek wisdom while bypassing the fear of the Lord is a fruitless endeavor.

2 - The fear of the Lord is the foundation upon which wisdom rests.

When we search and find wisdom, we discover, at its heart, the fear of the Lord. It is the root out of which the tree grows. In Proverbs 2:1-6, Solomon tells us how to search for wisdom. We are to "make our ear attentive" to it, "cry" for it, "seek her," "search for her as for hidden treasure." After diligent digging for wisdom, what do we discover? That's right. We "discern the fear of the Lord" (v. 5). Search diligently for wisdom as though mining treasure, and when we hit the mother lode, we will know that wisdom has its foundation in the fear of God.

Solomon not only declares this in Proverbs, but he also demonstrates it in Ecclesiastes. The Book of Ecclesiastes is the testimony of Solomon's search for wisdom. Wisdom, he found, was not to be discovered in wealth, power, comfort, pleasure, long life or scholarly pursuits. His findings are dearly presented as a summation to his book. What was the simple philosophy of this man who became legendary for his wisdom? *"The conclusion, when all has been heard, is: fear God and keep His commandments, because this applies to every person"* (Ecclesiastes 12:13).

3 - The fear of the Lord is the building block

out of which wisdom is constructed.

The fear of the Lord is the beginning of wisdom in the same way the ABC's are the beginning of the English language. To learn English we begin with the alphabet, learning the ABC's. No matter how proficient we become in the use of the English language we can never graduate from the use of A's, B's and C's. We just can't have English without them. To learn godly wisdom we must begin with the fear of the Lord. No matter how wise we become in the things of God, we can never graduate from the fear of the Lord, for the moment we depart from it we depart from wisdom as well.

Who, then, is the man that fears the LORD?
He will instruct him in the way chosen for him.
He will spend his days in prosperity, and his descendants will inherit the land. The LORD confides in those who fear him; he makes his covenant known to them.
Psalm 25:12-14 NIV

A Fountain of Life
"The fear of the LORD is a fountain of life." (Proverbs 14:27)

Godly wisdom will lead us to a fountain that flows with many of life's greatest delights. The Bible speaks about many blessed benefits that come to those who fear God. At first glance, things like comfort, joy, trust and peace seem to be incompatible with fear, but the verses listed below clearly connect the fear of the Lord to the consistent enjoyment of these and other blessings. I hope you will meditate on these Scripture passages and see how God has wedded holy fear with the happy benefits of being in covenant with Him. Walking in the fear of the Lord is like wading in a fountain. So come on in—the water's fine.

Fear and comfort
"So the church throughout all Judea and Galilee and Samaria enjoyed peace, being built up; and, going on in the fear of the Lord and in the comfort of the Holy Spirit, it continued to increase." (Acts 9:31)

Fear and joy
"So the women hurried away from the tomb, afraid yet filled with joy, and ran to tell his disciples."
(Matthew 28:8 NIV)

"Serve the LORD with fear and rejoice with trembling." (Psalm 2:11 NIV)

Fear and the assurance of forgiveness
"If you, O LORD, kept a record of sins, O Lord, who could stand? But with you there is forgiveness; therefore you are feared."

(Psalm 130:3-4 NIV)

Fear and praise
"You who fear the LORD, praise him! All you descendants of Jacob, honor him! Revere him, all you descendants of Israel!" (Psalm 22:23 NIV)

"And fear gripped them all, and they began glorifying God, saying, 'A great prophet has arisen among us!' and, 'God has visited His people!'" (Luke 7:16)

"And fear fell upon them all and the name of the Lord Jesus was being magnified." (Acts 19:17)

Fear and trust
"He put a new song in my mouth, a hymn of praise to our God. Many will see and fear and put their trust in the LORD." (Psalm 40:3 NIV)

Fear and worship
"Worship the LORD in the splendor of his holiness; tremble before him, all the earth." (Psalm 96:9 NIV)

Fear and hope
"Do not let your heart envy sinners, but always be zealous for the fear of the LORD. There is surely a future hope for you, and your hope will not be cut off." (Proverbs 23:17-18 NIV)

Fear and peace
"The fear of the LORD leads to life: then one rests content, untouched by trouble." (Proverbs 19:23 NIV)

Fear and delight
"Blessed is the man who fears the LORD, who finds great delight in his commands." (Psalm 112:1 NIV)

Fear and courage
"In the fear of the LORD there is strong confidence,..." (Proverbs 14:26)

> **In the fear of the Lord there is strong confidence.**

Fear and loving compassion
"For as high as the heavens are above the earth, so great is his love for those who fear him; as far as the east is from the west, so far has he removed our transgressions from us. As a father has compassion on his children, so the LORD has compassion on those who fear him." (Psalm 103:11-13 NIV)

Fear and contentment
"Do not let your heart envy sinners, but always be zealous for the fear of the LORD." (Proverbs 23:17 NIV)

Fear and progress in faith
"So then, my beloved, just as you have always obeyed, not as in

my presence only, but now much more in my absence, work out your salvation with fear and trembling; for it is God who is at work in you, both to will and to work for His good pleasure." (Philippians 2:12-13)

Fear and holiness

"For we are the temple of the living God; just as God said, 'I will dwell in them and walk among them; and I will be their God, and they shall be my people.' Therefore, come out from their midst and be separate, says the Lord. And do not touch what is unclean; and I will welcome you. And I will be a Father to you. And you shall be sons and daughters to Me,' says the Lord Almighty. Therefore, having these promises, beloved, let us cleanse ourselves from all defilement of flesh and spirit, perfecting holiness in the fear of God." (2 Corinthians 6:16-7:1)

Fear and good sleep

"The fear of the LORD leads to life, so that one may sleep satisfied, untouched by evil." (Proverbs 19:23)

Fear and honor

"The fear of the LORD is the instruction for wisdom, and before honor comes humility." (Proverbs 15:33)

Fear and guidance

"Who is the man who fears the LORD? He will instruct him in the way he should choose. His soul will abide in prosperity, and

his descendants will inherit the land. The secret of the LORD is for those who fear Him, and He will make them know His covenant." (Psalm 25:12-14)

"Who is among you that fears the LORD, that obeys the voice of his Servant, that walks in darkness and has no light? Let him trust in the name of the LORD and rely on his God." (Isaiah 50:10)

Fear and family prosperity

"Oh that they had such a heart in them, that they would fear Me, and keep all My commandments always, that it may be well with them and with their sons forever!" (Deuteronomy 5:29)

"Praise the LORD! How blessed is the man who fears the LORD, who greatly delights in His commandments. His descendants will be mighty on earth; The generation of the upright will be blessed. Wealth and riches are in his house, And his righteousness endures forever." "He will not fear evil tidings; His heart is steadfast, trusting in the LORD." (Psalm 112:1-3,7)

"How blessed is everyone who fears the LORD, Who walks in His ways. When you shall eat of the fruit of your hands, You will be happy and it will be well with you. Your wife shall be like a fruitful vine, Within your house, Your children like olive plants around your table. Behold, for thus shall the man be bless-

ed Who fears the LORD." (Psalm 128:1-4)

Fear and God's watchful care
"Then those who feared the LORD spoke to one another, and the LORD gave attention and heard it, and a book of remembrance was written before Him for those who fear the LORD and who esteem His name. 'And they will be Mine,' says the LORD of hosts, 'on the day that I prepare My own possession, and I will spare them as a man spares his own son who serves him.'" (Malachi 3:16-17)

Fear and answers to prayer
"Then they will call on me, but I will not answer; They will seek me diligently, but they shall not find me, Because they hated knowledge, And did not choose the fear of the LORD." (Proverbs 1:28-29)

"Who in the days of his flesh, when he [Jesus] had offered up prayers and supplications with strong crying and tears unto him that was able to save him from death, and was heard in that he feared." (Hebrews 5:7 KJV)

Fear and protection
"How great is Thy goodness, Which Thou hast stored up for those who fear Thee, Which Thou hast wrought for those who take refuge in Thee, Before the sons of men! Thou dost hide them in the secret place of Thy presence from the conspiracies of

man; Thou dost keep them secretly in a shelter from the strife of tongues." (Psalm 31:19-20)

"The angel of the LORD encamps around those who fear Him, And rescues them." (Psalm 34:7)

"Thou hast given a banner to those who fear Thee, That it may be displayed because of the truth. That Thy beloved may be delivered, Save with Thy right hand, and answer us!" (Psalm 60:4-5)

"It is the LORD of hosts whom you should regard as holy. And He shall be your fear, And He shall be your dread. Then He shall become a sanctuary; ..." (Isaiah 8:13-14)

Fear and salvation
"Surely His salvation is near to those who fear Him, That glory may dwell in our land." (Psalm 85:9)

Fear and long life
"The fear of the LORD prolongs life, but the years of the wicked will be shortened." (Proverbs 10:27)

"Although a sinner does evil a hundred times and may lengthen his life, still I know that it will be well for those who fear God, who fear Him openly. But it will not be well for the evil man and he will not lengthen his days like a shadow, because he does not

fear God." (Ecclesiastes 8:12-13)

Fear and healing
"But for you who fear My name the sun of righteousness will rise with healing in its wings; and you will go forth and skip about like calves from the stall." (Malachi 4:2)

Fear and mercy
"And His mercy is upon generation after generation towards the who fear Him." (Luke 1:50)

What wonderful promises are given to those who fear God! Of course the Bible is not teaching that if you have a healthy fear of God you will be without problems. Jesus himself said, "In this world you will have tribulation." Nor should we conclude that those who fear the Lord are immune from tragedy and disappointment.

The fact that someone dies young, has poor health, goes bankrupt or has an unhappy family life is not proof that they do not possess a healthy fear of the Lord. Nevertheless it remains true that robust reverence tends to enrich our lives in many ways and positions us to enjoy the life of blessing God has prepared for us.

O Lord, teach us to cultivate holy reverence and thus unlock the wealth of heaven's treasury.

Part 3
More than a Feeling

'Tis Grace Hath Brought Me Safe Thus Far and Grace Will Lead Me Home

Chapter Seven

Reverence in Our Hearts

Translating Precept into Practice

Jeffrey came to me and said, "Pastor, I think I'm beginning to understand what the fear of God is." I asked him to tell me about it. "Well," he replied, "I am going to have to be scrupulously honest in my business dealings, and I need to spend more time preparing my heart before I arrive for worship on Sundays, and…" As Jeffrey continued to tell me about the changes he needed to make in his life, I knew he had come to an important understanding. The fear of the Lord is more than a feeling. It is more than a concept with which to agree. It is a commitment to action.

A healthy fear of God will translate into practical expressions of godliness in our lives.

In the next four chapters we will explore the ways that an active commitment to fearing God will unleash transforming power in our hearts, our homes, our churches and our workplaces. First, let us examine how the commitment to fear the Lord has a wholesome, sanctifying effect upon our hearts.

Reverence in Our Hearts

The Bible consistently links the fear of the Lord with purity of heart. Albert Martin says, "The fear of the Lord is the soil out of which a godly life grows." When reverence for God is firmly in place, people are kinder and more honest. A fascinating example of this is found in one of the early laws of moral behavior given to the Israelites during Moses' term of leadership. *"You shall not curse a deaf man, nor place a stumbling block before the blind, but you shall revere your God; I am the LORD"* (Leviticus 19:14). A deaf man cannot hear a curse thrown his way. A blind man has no way of knowing who tripped him. They make perfect targets for mischievous bullies. Anyone pestering the deaf and the blind would not have to worry about being caught by his victims, so what would restrain him from inflicting pain upon them? According to Moses the knowledge that God is watching would be sufficient motivation to do what is right.

Much of today's Judeo-Christian ethic is based on the need to behave properly whether or not another person is observing us. Who we are in private is just as important as who we present ourselves to be in public. The certain awareness of God's presence everywhere will make us want to be as clean in thought and action when we are alone as when we are in public.

Conversely a community without reverence is a society that operates with little moral restraint. Nervousness about the possible lack of moral restraint in a nearby tribe led Abraham to make a drastic mistake and put his wife Sarah in serious jeopardy. In his nomadic travels, Abraham and his family came to Gerar, a district ruled by a man named Abimelech. Since Sarah was physically beautiful, Abraham was afraid that Abimelech would kill him in order to take Sarah as his wife. So Abraham claimed Sarah was only his sister, thinking that even if Abimelech took Sarah he might escape being murdered himself. As it turned out Abimelech did take Sarah to be his wife. However that night God appeared to Abimelech in a dream and said to him, *"Behold, you are a dead man because of the woman whom you have taken, for she is married"* (Genesis 20:3). Stricken with terror Abimelech wasted no time returning Sarah to her husband. When challenged as to why he had lied about being married to Sarah, Abraham explained, *"Because I thought, surely there is no fear of God in this place; and they will kill me because of my wife"* (Genesis 20:11). Though his cowardly conduct was inexcusable, Abraham was right to associate the absence of godly reverence with immoral behavior.

When Reverence Rules

I was 23 years old when I entered seminary to begin the theological training that helped prepare me to be a pastor. During those exciting years I was overjoyed to experience daily growth in my relationship with the Lord. For six years I had resisted the call of God before finally making the commitment to unreservedly live life His way. I had pursued joy while running from God, but now I discovered that by pursuing God, joy found me. Walking with God was nothing less than a thrilling adventure. While living in the men's dormitory on campus I took a part time job cleaning the bathrooms of the dorm. To my way of thinking, that is close to the bottom of the list when it comes to glamorous jobs. Nevertheless, to my surprise I found myself enjoying my work. I knew God saw my work and my goal was to please Him, so I did my best as I cleaned those bathrooms. Without my realizing it, reverence was moving me to put a high shine on every toilet in the place.

Whether we are talking about sanitizing toilets or sanctifying human hearts, one of the most powerful cleansing agents we have at our disposal is the fear of the Lord. John approached me in the parking lot of a rural church where I was speaking. "Last night God did something significant in the life of my son," he said. His son Billy was 15 years old. The previous evening Billy had heard me teach about the fear of the Lord and prayed for God to bring holy fear into his life. "It was what happened next that surprised me," continued John. "Billy came to me when we got home and described how he had recently become attracted to pornography, but when he became serious about seeking the fear of the Lord somehow he knew he would have to walk away from this dehumanizing practice. 'Dad, would you come outside with me? Let's burn this stuff.'" Together they destroyed the magazines and committed themselves to walk in purity. It should not surprise us that the fear of the Lord affects the level of holiness in our lives. The simple truth is that reverence for God makes us better people.

Wise King Solomon said, *"...by the fear of the LORD men depart from evil"* (Proverbs 16:6 KJV). He knew that people require assistance to walk away from evil and he identified the fear of the Lord as the very thing we need to be able to break sin's grip. Just because we reject sin does not mean that sin will release us. Even when we determine to refuse dishonesty, greed, pride, sloth, gluttony, bitterness, hatred, gossip, lust, jealousy, and strife, such evils can remain influential in our lives. Once within us they have a strong hold on us and we find ourselves unable to shake free from them without powerful help. Reverence for God is just the help we need in the battle against unholiness. When reverence rules in the human heart, goodness overcomes evil.

The Apostle Paul knew what it was to experience transformation toward goodness. The theological term for growth in godliness is sanctification. Much of Paul's writing in the New Testament deals with sanctification—the process of becoming like Christ. Frequently he encouraged believers to pursue excellence in character. At one point he expressed it this way: *"...beloved, let us cleanse ourselves from all defilement of flesh and spirit, perfecting holiness in the fear of God"* (2 Corinthians

7:1). Like Solomon, Paul understood that the fear of God is essential to overcoming sin.

When I began to actively embrace the fear of the Lord in the mid 1980's, I noticed that some sins loosened their hold on me. I began experiencing a stronger sanctifying influence over sins that previously I had had limited and inconsistent victory in overcoming. Proverbs 16:6 was becoming my reality. By the fear of the Lord I was departing from evil. Reverence reigned where sin had ruled my life. Lust loosened its grip. Faith dislodged unbelief. Diligence supplanted sloth. Christ routed self from my heart's throne and took His rightful place at the center of my life. Never had I felt so free! Holy reverence made it clear that life is not so much about me as it is about my awesome Lord.

"Therefore do not let sin reign in your mortal body that you should obey its lusts, and do not go on presenting the members of your body to sin as instruments of unrighteousness; but present yourselves to God as those alive from the dead, and your members as instruments of righteousness to God" (Romans 6:12-13). Sin is stronger than we are, but godly reverence gives us access to a resource that is sufficient to break sin's grip and places us in the loving hands of our Creator God, who rules in majesty.

Chapter Eight

Reverence in Our Homes

God designed family life. It is no wonder then that those who honor God with holy reverence experience His active involvement in the establishment and enrichment of their homes. Remember Shiphrah and Puah, the midwives in Egypt described in an earlier chapter? By means of the fear of God they found courage to disobey Pharaoh's law and spared the life of the newborn Moses. As a result God rewarded these brave women. *"And it came about because the midwives feared God, that He established households for them"* (Exodus 1:21). God established homes for them. To establish means to "set securely in a position of strength." Many who follow the Lord find Him at work in their homes. Two of the Psalms describe the benefits enjoyed by the families of those who fear God.

Praise the LORD!
How blessed is the man who fears the LORD, Who greatly delights in His commandments. His descendants will be mighty on earth; The generation of the upright will be blessed. Wealth and riches are in his house,
And his righteousness endures forever. Light arises in the darkness for the upright;
He is gracious and compassionate and righteous.
It is well with the man who is gracious and lends;
He will maintain his cause in judgment. For he will never be shaken;
The righteous will be remembered forever.
Psalm 112:1-6

How blessed is everyone who fears the LORD,
Who walks in His ways.
When you shall eat of the fruit of your hands,
You will be happy and it will be well with you.
Your wife shall be like a fruitful vine, Within your house,
Your children like olive plants Around your table.
Behold, for thus shall the man be blessed Who fears the LORD.
Psalm 128:1-4

Reverence and Marriage

One of the most important issues in family life is the bond between husband and wife. Scripture gives striking descriptions of the intimacy of heart that God intends for couples who have been joined in marriage. Inherent in this intimacy is reverence for God and reverence for our mates, which the Bible identifies as key factors in the success of a marriage:

- Reverence unites our hearts so that our marital union becomes spiritual as well as physical. *"...I will give them one heart and one way, that they may fear Me..."* (Jeremiah 32:39)
- Reverence for Christ enables us to willingly place ourselves at the disposal of our mates. *"Be subject to one another in the fear of Christ."* (Ephesians 5:21)
- Reverence motivates us to seek our partner's highest good even if doing so costs us dearly. *"Nevertheless, let every one of you in particular so love his wife even as himself; and the wife see that she reverence her husband."* (Ephesians 5:33 KJV)

Holy Fear Blesses Our Children

"I will give them one heart and one way, that they may fear Me always, for their own good, and for the good of their children after them." (Jeremiah 32:39)

As parents our greatest fears may have more to do with the lives of our children than with ourselves, as this mother's story reveal . She was the mother of two girls. One was twenty-two years old and the other was ten. Her twenty-two year-old had been living in rebellion against her parents and her Lord. This mother was afraid that her older daughter would not return to a life of faithfulness. She also worried that her younger daughter might follow her older sister's example. Having heard me teach about the Lord's willingness to break the power of unhealthy fears in our lives, she asked, "Does the Bible have anything to say about my fear?"

It's a good question. What about those fears to which we as parents are frequently subject? Nothing thrills parents more than to see their children living godly and blessed lives. Nothing disturbs believing parents more than to watch as a child rushes down a path that is sure to bring heartache and pain. Are there any assurances for parents who are trying to raise their children in a dangerous world, filled with moral landmines and spiritual booby traps? The good news is that the Biblical teachings on the fear of the Lord apply very directly to the challenging task of rearing godly children in an ungodly world.

A Father's Legacy

A story in the Old Testament illustrates the commitment God has made to care for the children of those who fear Him. The story takes place during the ministry of the prophet Elisha and centers around one of Elisha's servants. The facts about this young servant's life are scarce. We know he was a preacher's son. We know he died before his time, leaving behind a distraught wife and two young boys. We know he "feared the Lord." In ancient Israel a widow could find herself hard pressed to keep her family together when the breadwinner died. Employment opportunities for women were nonexistent and government welfare programs were still just a gleam in a yet to be born bureaucrat's eye.

However, many years earlier God had revealed His commitment to care for the children of those who feared Him. On the day He gave the Ten Commandments God said, *"Oh that they had such a heart in them, that they would fear Me, and keep all my commandments always, that it may be well with them and with their sons forever"* (Deuteronomy 5:29). God promised to bring good to the children of God-fearing parents. So when this young student-prophet embraced the fear of the Lord, he secured divine blessings for his sons. The day came when death ended his opportunity to provide for his family himself. So the Lord moved heaven and earth to secure the welfare of this young man's family. It's really quite a story.

> *Now a certain woman of the wives of the sons of the prophets cried out to Elisha, 'Your servant my husband is dead, and you know that your servant feared the LORD; and the creditor has come to take my two children to be his slaves.' And Elisha said to her, 'What shall I do for you? Tell me, what do you have in the house?' And she said, 'Your maidservant has nothing in the house except a jar of oil.' Then he said, 'Go, borrow vessels at large for yourself from all your neighbors, even empty vessels; do not get a few. And you shall go in and shut the door behind you and your sons, and pour out into all these vessels; and you shall set aside what is full.' So she went from him and shut the door behind her and her sons; they were bringing the vessels to her and she poured. And it came about when the vessels were full, that she said to her son, 'Bring me another vessel.' And he said to her, 'There is not one vessel more.' And the oil stopped. Then she came and told the man of God. And he said, 'Go, sell the oil and pay your debt, and you and your sons can live on the rest.'*
> 2 Kings 4:1-7

Although our children need things that we do not have the ability to give them, their security does not have to be limited by our strength or availabili-

God is strong in His support of the offspring of those who fear Him.

ty. When this young father came to the end of what he could do, God provided for his family, far beyond what he had been able to do during his lifetime. One of the wellsprings of blessings that flow from the fear of the Lord is the wonderful impact it has on our children. God is strong in His support of the offspring of those who fear Him. It follows that one of the most important things a parent can do to bless his children is to embrace the holy fear of the Lord.

In Moses' day God voiced His desire that His people fear Him. He said that reverence and obedience would cause life to *"go well with them and with their sons forever"* (Deuteronomy 5:29). When Jehovah promised the new covenant He vowed He would give His people a heart to fear Him. He made it clear that this was *"for their own good and the good of their children after them"* (Jeremiah 32:39). God has committed Himself in three specific ways to the strong support of the children of those who fear Him.

1. Sufficiency. *"Who is the man who fears the LORD? He will instruct him in the way he should choose. His soul will abide in prosperity, And his descendants will inherit* *the land"* (Psalm 25:12-13). Worldwide, many live in poverty. God's promise of land is in essence a promise of sufficiency. The key to giving our children sufficiency is not found in amassing a large bank balance. It is best secured by our faithful cultivation of the holy fear of the Lord.

2. **Strength.** *"How blessed is the man who fears the LORD, Who greatly delights in His commandments. His descendants will be mighty on earth;..."* (Psalm 112:1-2). Our children's success in life will require an adequate measure of physical, moral and spiritual strength. Here God promises "might" to the offspring of people who fear Him.

3. **Security.** *"In the fear of the LORD there is strong confidence, And his children will have refuge"* (Proverbs 14:26). This world is sometimes a stormy place, but the children of those who fear God will have refuge.

Many parents spend a major part of their lives and efforts attempting to secure the future for their children. They may accumulate large estates, seeking to protect their children from want in a world where many lack the basics. They carefully oversee the health and development of their children, hoping to imbue them with strength to face whatever comes their way. They try to shield them from stresses and storms, wishing to safeguard them from the distresses and dangers that haunt human experience. How comforting to know that by embracing the holy fear of God, we can insure God's action on behalf of our children and that He will do more for them than we could ever do ourselves.

Chapter Nine

Reverence in the Church

A healthy church has a healthy fear of God that transforms the life and work of that church. Multiple passages in the New Testament combine to give us a picture of the salutary impact of godly reverence on the life and work of the church.

The Impact of Holy Fear on Worship

Worship is the single most important activity of the church. Styles and formats of worship vary from congregation to congregation. God seems to delight in these diverse expressions of love offered to Him, but there is one quality that God requires in every experience of public or private worship. Without this quality, worship degenerates into religious ritual that is devoid of spiritual life. Such empty worship is unacceptable to God. In one case God struck dead two irreverent worshipers, saying, *"...By those who come near Me I will be treated as holy,..."* (Leviticus 10:1-3).[1] The essential quality required by God in worship is reverence. In fact reverence and worship are so inextricably bound together that the terms for worshiping God and fearing God are sometimes used interchangeably in the Bible. For example, in 2 Kings 17 and Joshua 22:25 the King James Version consistently renders the Hebrew word *yare* as fear. When the translation committee for the New International Version came to the same passages, they translated *yare* as worship. Did they make a mistake? Not at all. The Hebrew word conveys both concepts. In this context the phrase *"and taught them how they should **fear** the LORD"* (KJV) has the meaning *"and taught them how to **worship** the LORD"* (NIV emphasis added). See 2 Kings 17:28.

Hebrews 12:28-29 (NIV) calls our attention to the worship we offer to God. *"Therefore, since we are receiving a kingdom that cannot be shaken, let us be thankful, and so worship God acceptably with reverence and awe, for our 'God is a consuming fire.'"* The New Testament writer spends a good portion of this chapter writing about the nature of worship. In verses 18-29 he compares the worship of the ancient Jews with the nature of Christian worship inaugurated by Jesus. He begins by reminding his readers that their forefathers' worship of Jehovah at Mount Sinai was such an awesome encounter with God that the people *"begged that no further word should be spoken to them."* Even Moses said, *"I am full of fear and trembling."*

He goes on to explain that worship under the new covenant is different, but certainly no less awesome. Every time a Christian enters into genuine worship he approaches an incredible kingdom of unfathomable dimension and immeasurable power. The fact that this kingdom is unseen by the worshiper does not make it unreal. There is only one acceptable posture for us to take in light of this reality. We must offer worship *"with reverence and awe, for our God is a consuming fire."*

Reverent worship recognizes the Presence of the Holy One in our midst. Reverent worship replaces our self-importance with larger kingdom issues. Reverent worship engages our energies in active and complete submission to the Divine agenda of redemption. Reverent worship opens our ears to hear as disciples and seals our commitment to serve without reservation. Reverent worship captures the passion of our hearts and directs it toward His highest purpose. No wonder Jesus said that the Father is seeking those who will worship Him in spirit and in truth. Worship is about spiritual realities. It can only be understood by spiritual beings engaging in spiritual communion with the Creator, who Himself is spirit. Ritual that ignores this standard is subject to judgment by the One who defined worship in the first place. How foolish it would be to neglect mental and moral preparation and to barge in, brashly demanding center stage. Come boldly? Yes! Come joyfully? Yes! But come clothed in humility and reverent fear.

The Impact of Holy Fear on Preaching and Teaching.

No preacher in ancient or modern times has surpassed the Apostle Paul in depth or influence. He has provided inspiration for those of every generation who have stood to preach the gospel of Jesus Christ. His methods and content have been explored thoroughly. Yet one of the integral qualities of his preaching often goes overlooked. When describing his preaching ministry to the Corinthian Christians, Paul revealed a surprising fact. *"I was with you in weakness and in fear and in much trembling"* (1 Corinthians 2:3).

Many public speakers have experienced stage fright,

but Paul was pinpointing something entirely different from nervousness at the prospect of standing before a crowd. The fear he felt had nothing to do with worries about his performance or the reaction of his audience. He was not anxious lest something he said offended an important personage or decreased the size of the weekly offering. Paul was not intimidated by such matters. His fear was not prompted by the ones <u>before</u> whom he stood. Rather it was a result of his keen awareness of the One <u>for</u> whom he stood. This becomes clear when we examine the statement immediately preceding his confession of weakness, fear and trembling: *"For I determined to know nothing among you except Jesus Christ, and Him crucified"* (1 Corinthians 2:2).

> **We need preachers who are so filled with awe concerning God and their responsibility toward Him that they lose their fear of people.**

The reason Paul experienced weakness and fear was because his attention was on "Jesus Christ and Him crucified." His reverence toward God made him bold before men and women. We need preachers who are so filled with awe concerning God and their responsibility toward Him that they lose their fear of people. If a preacher's goal is to please people, he will shape the message to fit what he thinks they want. He will focus on what is popular with his audience instead of what is profitable for them. In doing so, he will substitute the wisdom of men for the power of God.

No preacher is going to please everyone who hears him. Some to whom he speaks are immature. Some are saints. Some are selfish. Some are skeptics. Some are sincere souls who want to hear from God. Others just want their ears tickled. Since he can't please all of them, a preacher must be selective in choosing someone to please. The wise preacher will play to an audience of One, seeking to please the Lord who called and commissioned him. The opinion that counts is the opinion of *"...the One who impartially judges according to each man's work." Therefore "conduct yourselves in fear during the time of your stay upon earth; ..."* (1 Peter 1:17). One of the evidences of the need for restoration of the fear of the Lord in our churches is the quickness with which many will speak for God even though they have not heard from Him. Jeremiah delivered the Lord's rebuke to those who had not heard from God, but claimed to speak for Him. *"Therefore,' declares the LORD, 'I am against the prophets who steal from one another words supposedly from me. Yes,' declares the LORD, 'I am against the prophets who wag their own tongues and yet declare, 'The LORD declares.' Indeed, I am against those who prophesy false dreams,' declares the LORD. 'They tell them and lead my people astray with their reckless lies, yet I did not send or appoint them. They do not benefit these people in the least,' declares the LORD."* (Jeremiah 23:30-32 NIV). Contrast these reckless religionists with those faithful prophets whose *"bones tremble...because of the Lord"* (verse 9). They were the ones who *"stood in the council of the LORD to see or to hear his word"* (verse 18). They were extremely careful to deliver God's messages exactly as they had received them and never, never to claim they had a message from God when they did not. Those who speak without having heard from God do not benefit the people who hear them. Rather, they lead them astray. *"But if they had stood in my council, they would have proclaimed my words to my people and would have turned them from their evil ways and from their evil deeds"* (verse 22 NIV). Even Jesus refused to speak on his own initiative saying, *"For I did not speak of my own accord, but the Father who sent me commanded me what to say and how to say it. I know that his command leads to eternal life. So whatever I say is just what the Father has told me to say"* (John 12:49-50 NIV). A healthy fear of the Lord will insure integrity and accuracy in handling the word of God.

The Impact of Holy Fear on Evangelism.

The church has good news! God is reconciling the world to Himself in Christ. He has given the church the ministry of reconciliation and the words that will effect that reconciliation. (See 2 Corinthians 5:18-21) This ministry is evangelism, which means to broadcast good news. When a church lacks a healthy fear of God, one of the things that suffers is the ability to effectively bring to people the good news of what God is doing.

There are at least three ways in which a proper awe of God will strengthen the work of evangelism.

First, the fear of God steadies the resolve of the evangelist (2 Corinthians 5:11). Evangelism does not come easily for most of us. To stand and speak words of reconciliation provokes negative reactions from those who do not like the message. This reaction can range from simple rudeness to violent persecution. Few Christians enjoy generating the hostility that the gospel can provoke from unbelievers. So what makes us do it when we know that it may engender a negative response? Paul explained his motivation in 2 Corinthians 5:10-11. *"We must all appear before the judgment-seat of Christ, that each one may be recompensed for his deeds in the body, according to what he has done, whether good or bad. Therefore knowing the fear of the Lord, we persuade men,..."* He knew that judgment, serious and sobering, would come. Realizing the awesomeness of the Judge and the judgment process, Paul was highly motivated to persuade every person to find the grace and forgiveness that prepares for eternity. He accepted the cost of speaking his faith because he knew that one day he would stand before the judgment seat of Christ, as would every man, woman and child who heard him speak. His reverence for the One who sits in judgment led him to do all in his power to prepare himself and others for that day.

Second, the quality of reverent fear gives strength to the message of reconciliation (1 Peter 3:1-2). Some things speak louder than words. Peter counseled wives who wished to encourage their husbands. Some were married to men who were disobedient to God and these wives wanted to influence their husbands to turn to God. Few men are prone to gracefully accept preaching from their wives. So, Peter pointed to two qualities in the lives of these women that would speak louder and more effectively than words. Those two qualities were moral purity and reverent fear of God. *"…they may be won over without words by the behavior of their wives, when they see the purity and reverence of your lives."*

Third, the fear of Lord awakens those outside the church to their need for God (Acts 5:11-14). When two church members lied to God, His judgment came

When the fear of the Lord grips a community, many are drawn to God. swiftly. Both were struck dead and great fear electrified the church. As the news spread, those outside the church also feared, impressed with the fact that no one could deceive or hide from the God of the Christians. We might expect this to kill the effectiveness of any evangelism program in the church, but it had the opposite effect. *"And all the more believers in the Lord, multitudes of men and women, were constantly added to their number."* It is true that when the fear of the Lord grips a community, many are drawn to God by that fear and are incorporated into the church. When the people of God set out to evangelize others, they are wise to pray for a holy fear of God within the church and in the communities they are trying to reach.

The Impact of Holy Fear on Revival.

Many are praying for the revival of today's church. The fear of the Lord is a match that is lighting revival fires across the globe. In Acts 19 we have an account of one of the most extraordinary revivals in the history of Christianity. Revival so transformed the city of Ephesus that this major metropolis was converted from a center of pagan worship into the heart of one of the most influential Christian churches the world has seen. Much of the New Testament was written to or from Ephesus. It served as a home base for such great leaders as Timothy and the Apostle John. I believe the match that lighted these revival fires can be identified in one phrase found in verse 17. *"And fear fell upon them all."*

For years the church that I pastored in Texas verged on revival, but fears held us back—fear of the unknown, fear of losing control, fear of what others would think. On the morning after God confronted me with His holy fear in 1985, I stood to preach to the congregation. I knew that God's touch the night before had changed my life, but I did not suspect how it would affect those gathered for worship that day. As I concluded the sermon, a strange sound came from the congregation. At first I did not know what I was hearing. Then it dawned on me. It was the sound of wailing. I don't think I had ever heard a group wail before. Certainly it had never happened in the sophisticated, upper middle class congregation I pastored. Quickly the front of the auditorium filled with people. They left their seats to find places near the altar and to prostrate themselves before God. Many wept. Some confessed sin or cried to God for mercy. Many requested prayer.

I was astonished by this event, but those who are familiar with the history of revival know that holy fear has been a common characteristic of the outpouring of God's Spirit upon His church in every age and culture since Christ founded the church. Dr. Wesley Duewel, a former president of OMS International, is the author of a wonderful history of revival entitled Revival Fire in which he documents revival movements of God around the world. Dr. Duewel points out that *"revival converts tend to be lasting converts. They have a permanent reverential awe of God and an abiding love for Christ."*[2] (Italics mine.) Revivals in Africa, Asia, Europe, North and South America share the common thread that whenever God has visited His church in powerful grace, holy fear has been a blessed bond uniting the hearts of believers to the heart of the Lord.

After I taught a seminar on the fear of the Lord in the Philippines, one pastor wrote, describing the difference that embracing the fear of God had made in his life. Here is his story in his own words.

Before the seminar I was already burdened as a pastor and as a person in general. I felt that I was doing a bad job and ought to resign soon. I had already prayed to God to remove me from my pastorate because I was a poor representative of the Kingdom.

I just wanted to quit. During the seminar I was immediately drawn to the necessity of fear. In my younger days, the fear of God had a special place in my heart but it died down. Then when I heard you speak on it, I felt that desire reawakened. I sat in my seat and exclaimed, "How true!"

The following Sundays were different. I was feeling God was speaking to me and that He wanted me to do something unusual in the church service. I could almost hear Him saying what I should do. God wanted me to make an altar call. I normally don't do that kind of thing because I'm ashamed and I don't know how. At the close of my message I did the unthinkable for me. I gave an altar call. I didn't even want to look at the congregation, but when I opened my eyes they were in front and crying. God must have pushed them real hard! And the complexion of our church began to change. We were actually experiencing revival joy.

Many churches are rediscovering the importance of cultivating the fear of the Lord and in the process they are experiencing empowerment for worship, preaching, teaching, evangelism and revival. Like the first century church, congregations today are blessed when they embrace the greater fear.

"So the church throughout all Judea and Galilee and Samaria enjoyed peace, being built up; and, going on in the fear of the Lord and in the comfort of the Holy Spirit, it continued to increase." Acts 9:31

---

[1] See also Acts 5:1-10 and 1 Corinthians 11:30 for examples of God's severe judgment upon irreverence in worship.

[2] Wesley Duewel, Revival Fire (Grand Rapids: Zondervan Publishing House, 1995), P. 13

Chapter Ten

Reverence in the Workplace

When we moved from the city to the country, our Dalmatian went into sensory overdrive. New and mysterious sights and sounds begged to be explored and Lady was eager to take it all in at once. But unknown dangers lurked in places our city dog could not imagine. She had spent her young life in an urban backyard, cut off from the outside world by a six-foot high wooden fence. It quickly became apparent that her heady reaction to this newfound freedom could cost Lady her life. The most immediate danger was the state highway that passed in front of the house. When we saw her response to the massive trucks and speeding cars, we knew we had a problem. Lady had no fear of traffic. After several near misses we had to take action. We fenced her in. We knew that her opportunities to explore the world would have to be severely restricted until she gained some healthy fear.

Healthy fear is not just good for a dog near a highway. It is also good for us. There are many exciting possibilities for achievement and significance, but a lack of healthy fear can lead our Heavenly Father to lovingly restrict our opportunities in this world. When God takes this action it is for our good. Once we have learned to embrace the healthy fear of God, He is able to entrust us with greater freedoms and we position ourselves to enjoy expanding potential in the workplace.

How does the fear of the Lord enhance our career experiences? According to Scripture there are some direct parallels between positive experiences in the marketplace and holy fear.

1 - Career Guidance

One of the ways reverence for God shapes our work is in the area of career guidance. Israel's King David is a stellar model of success in a career path. His reverence for God set his course and steadied his resolve as he pursued his life's work.

One of the songs he wrote describes the relationship between fearing God and selecting a career. *"Who, then, is the man that fears the LORD? He will instruct him in the way chosen for him. He will spend his days in prosperity, and his descendants will inherit the land. The LORD confides in those who fear him; he makes his covenant known to them"* (Psalm 25:12-14 NIV). To discover God's will in regard to life's work and to submit to that will is critical to achieving God-given potential in life.

The Bible tells us that God has work for us to do. In fact, He prepares our work beforehand and we are responsible to conform to the pattern of His preparation on our behalf. *"For we are His workmanship, created in Christ Jesus for good works, which God prepared beforehand, that we should walk in them"* (Ephesians 2:10). When we have healthy fear of God we will not allow anything less than God to set or alter our course. Reverence gives us the patience to wait for dear direction from the Lord in finding the work He has prepared for us. Once we enter the career He has chosen for us, reverence leads us to steady resolve and resistance to pressures that might otherwise force us to resign our assignment.

2 - Job Performance

The character trait of reverence tends to increase two important qualities in our attitude toward work. The first is energy and the second is integrity. Those who possess the healthy fear of the Lord tend to throw themselves wholeheartedly into their work. When Paul gave advice to slaves in the city of Colossae he did not advocate slavery, but he did demonstrate the connection between hard work and reverence for the Lord. *"Slaves, obey your earthly masters in everything; and do it, not only when their eye is on you and to win their favor, but with sincerity of heart and reverence for the Lord. Whatever you do, work at it with all your heart, as working for the Lord, not for men,..."* (Colossians 3:22-23 NIV). Indeed healthy fear of God promotes the energetic discharge of duties whether a supervisor is looking or not because we know that God sees and judges. Our relationship to Him motivates us to do our best. *"Since you call on a Father who judges each man's work impartially, live your lives as strangers here in reverent fear"* (1 Peter 1: 17 NIV).

However, it takes more than diligence for a person to have a positive influence on society through the workplace. Honesty is needed as well. Hard work may insure that we go far, but integrity enables us to proceed in the right direction. The quality of godly reverence encourages the kind of excellence in business practices that produces positive benefits for all.

Nehemiah understood this important link between the fear of the Lord and integrity. When he undertook rebuilding Jerusalem, the economy was in shambles and families were scrambling to survive. Many desperate fathers mortgaged their possessions and even indentured their family members in order to obtain something to eat. At that time some unscrupulous businessmen were profiting from the misery of their fellow countrymen by loaning out money at exorbitant rates. The practice of usury was financially profitable but morally bankrupt and Nehemiah challenged these men publicly. He appealed to them to return to the fear of God and abandon using hard times as an opportunity to gouge their neighbors. *"…The thing which you are doing is not good; should you not walk in the fear of our God because of the reproach of the nations, our enemies? And likewise I, my brothers and my servants, are lending them money and grain. Please, let us leave off this usury. Please, give back to them this very day their fields, their vineyards, their olive groves, and their houses, also the hundredth part of the money and of the grain, the new wine, and the oil that you are exacting from them"* (Nehemiah 5:9-11). To their credit these businessmen followed Nehemiah's counsel and let the fear of the Lord shape their business practices once again.

Today a loss of the fear of God has the same effect that it did centuries ago—it increases indolence and destroys integrity. We not only enrich ourselves but also our society when we "walk in the fear of our God" in our workplace.

3 - Leadership and Advancement

Historically, those who fear God have held key positions in their communities. When Moses' father-in-law Jethro advised Moses on the selection of judges to rule in Israel, he gave this counsel: *"But select capable men from all the people—men who fear God, trustworthy men who hate dishonest gain—and appoint them as officials over thousands, hundreds, fifties and tens"* (Exodus 18:21 NIV). One of the things that qualified these men for leadership was the fear of the Lord.

Nehemiah also looked for God-fearing men when he set out to fill leadership positions. *"I put in charge of Jerusalem my brother Hanani, along with Hananiah the commander of the citadel, because he was a man of integrity and feared God more than most men do"* (Nehemiah 7:2 NIV).

The Wisdom Literature of the Old Testament depicts a woman who succeeds in retail marketing: *"Charm is deceptive, and beauty is fleeting; but a woman who fears the LORD is to be praised. Give her the reward she has earned and let her works bring her praise at the city gate"* (Proverbs 31:30-31 NIV). The city gates were centers of buying and selling and places where contracts were made. So when the scripture speaks of work that brings praise at the city gate, financial achievement is implied. *"Humility and the fear of the LORD bring wealth and honor and life"* (Proverbs 22:4 NIV).

The prophet Daniel pursued a career in civil service. As a government employee Daniel served in the administration of three kings. He never bowed to their gods, but sometime during the reign of each, these three kings declared that the God of Daniel was supreme over all. His stellar success can in large measure be attributed to his holy fear of God. His own description of one encounter with the divine gives us a glimpse of how deeply his life was grounded in reverent fear. *"I, Daniel, was the only one who saw the vision; the men with me did not see it, but such terror overwhelmed them that they fled and hid themselves. So I was left alone, gazing at this great vision; I had no strength left, my face turned deathly pale and I was helpless. Then I heard him speaking, and as I listened to him, I fell into a deep sleep, my face to the ground. A hand touched me and set me trembling on my hands and knees. He said, 'Daniel, you who are highly esteemed, consider carefully the words I am about to speak to you, and stand up, for I have now been sent to you.' And when he said this to me, I stood up trembling"* (Daniel 10:7-11 NIV).

I have a friend who is a pharmacist in rural Oklahoma. A few years ago while working in a small pharmacy, he was faced with a moral dilemma on the job. He knew that if he did the right thing it could cost him his job, but his fear of God was stronger than his fear of unemployment so he made the moral choice. Indeed his employer quickly terminated his job. To the casual observer it would appear my friend was suddenly without a career, but God honors those who honor Him and soon his career grew in amazing fashion. "Even in my most optimistic faith I could not have imagined how these past seven years would play out," he says. Today he is the sole owner of a very successful pharmacy. In addition God has given him a remarkable platform as a leader in shaping policies for rural health care in pharmacies and hospitals across the nation. He moved from being employed in one pharmacy to beneficially influencing thousands of rural health care professionals and the countless customers they serve.

God is committed to the career advancement of those who fear Him. Whether we look to the example of Moses, Nehemiah, the Proverbs woman, Daniel, or my pharmacist friend, the constant at work is that *"Humility and the fear of the LORD bring wealth and honor and life"* (Proverbs 22:4 NIV).

4 - Good Employer/Employee Relationships

The Apostle Paul wrote to people from many stations in life. In one of his letters he called on slaves and their masters to treat each other with mutual respect, sincerity and kindness.

"Slaves, obey your earthly masters with respect and fear, and with sincerity of heart... And masters, treat your slaves in the same way. Do not threaten them, since you know that he who is both their Master and yours is in heaven, and there is no favoritism with him" (Ephesians 6:5-9 NIV). I do not think that Paul condoned or promoted slavery in this passage, rather he provided instruction in the Christian work ethic. Paul directs his counsel to two groups, those in authority and those under authority. His advice to labor was the same as to management: let the fear of God shape your relationship with one another so that your actions please your Father in heaven and you work toward the highest good for your brother on earth. For employer/employee relationships to work to the mutual benefit of both, they must begin in the holy fear of the Lord.

5 - Bountiful compensation

A final subject for consideration when exploring the effects of the fear of God on career is the pay package. Compensation paid by earthly employers is rarely all we hope it will be. However, there is good news for us when we determine to let the fear of the Lord shape our approach to our work. The consistent teaching of the Bible is that God rewards those who fear Him. Payment is not always in the currency of this world, but there is no doubt that those who fear the Lord will be rich in many ways. Psalm 112 describes the rich quality of life that becomes the heritage enjoyed by those who fear the Lord, as do the following verses:

"Fear the LORD, you his saints, for those who fear him lack nothing." "Come, my children, listen to me; I will teach you the fear of the LORD. Whoever of you loves life and desires to see many good days" (Psalm 34:9,11-12 NIV).

"He provides food for those who fear him; he remembers his covenant forever" (Psalm 111:5 NIV).

"Blessed are all who fear the LORD, who walk in his ways. You will eat the fruit of your labor; blessings and prosperity will be yours" (Psalm 128:1-2 NIV).

Wise people understand that the fear of the Lord is not to be compartmentalized as though it were a quality that is appropriate for religious life but has no place in the marketplace. They know that the greater fear is meant for every walk of life. For us who are willing to embrace this holy fear, God can take down the fences that limit our opportunities and trust us with the thrill of expanded horizons and fruitful labors.

Chapter 11

Reverence in Our Relationships

Bret Ellard, LPC

As a result of my work with individuals and families as a Christian counselor, I have gained an appreciation over the years for the important role trust plays in relationships. While I have observed that trusting those who are not trustworthy can have dire consequences, it seems equally problematic to fail to trust those who are trustworthy. As we consider what impact a healthy and holy fear of the Lord can have on our relationships, I would like to offer up this suggestion. I believe when properly understood, the biblical concept of the fear of the Lord should include the idea of fearing the failure to trust Him. If one is graced with a healthy fear of God, it would naturally follow that what God would have to say on a matter would be of supreme importance to that person. If one concludes that God is trustworthy, then failing to trust him should strike fear in our hearts. This fear of failing to trust God would drive us to further develop the manifestation of trusting him.

The cart (pleasing God) must always follow the horse (trusting God). While many Christians spend the greater portion of their lives seeking to please God, John Lynch suggests that "trusting God with who He says we are" is the more appropriate path to take. He references Hebrews 11:6, *"And without faith it is impossible to please God, for anyone who comes to God must believe that He is who He is and that He is a rewarder of those who diligently seek him."* (NIV). This passage reveals that the cart (pleasing God) must always follow the horse (trusting God). According to scripture, one cannot please God who does not trust him. And having the wisdom to trust God is born out of possessing a healthy and righteous fear of Him.

The late Gary Smalley observed, "life is relationships; the rest is just details." This highly acclaimed

Christian counselor and prolific writer spent his life seeking to strengthen and enhance relationships to be all they could be under God's design. We might well understand why, someone who devoted so much time to the issue of healthy personal relationships would place such emphasis on the topic. Yet, long before Smalley's quote, a Nazarene carpenter centuries earlier had emphasized the importance of relationships in a person's life. In fact, his thoughts were revealed in the context of his enemies' attempt to lure him into a trap, ironically to show his ignorance of the law. Recorded in Matthew's gospel we find the Pharisees sending one of their scholars of the law to Jesus and posing the question, *"Teacher, which is the greatest commandment in the law?" Jesus replied, "Love the Lord your God with all your heart, with all your soul, and with all your mind. This is the first and greatest commandment. And the second is like it: love your neighbor as yourself. All the law and the prophets hang on these two commandments."* (Matthew 22:36-40, NIV) Jesus, when asked about what matters most in life from God's perspective, answered by saying "loving God, loving others, and loving yourself." His answer suggests that a person's relationships with God, others, and him or herself are of primary concern for the Creator. In addition, love is emphasized as the major focus of these relationships. In short, based on Jesus's reply, Smalley is right, having observed that "life is relationships; the rest is just details."

Knowing that a healthy fear of God naturally leads to a deepening fear of failing to trust Him, let's consider what He has to say about relationships, knowing his guidance for relationships is altogether trustworthy. The remainder of this chapter seeks to explore important qualities that God desires us, as individuals, to possess in the context of our relationships. These attributes include, but are not limited to graciousness, truthfulness, courage, gentleness, and respect.

Being Gracious in Relationships.

John, the beloved apostle wrote of Jesus in connection with His incarnation, *"The Word became flesh and made His dwelling among us. We have seen His glory, the glory as of the one and only Son, full of grace and truth."* (John 1:14 NIV) Jesus revealed His graciousness in relationships throughout his earthly life. To be gracious carries the idea of being slow to take offense and subsequently slow to get angry. While anger is a naturally occurring emotion when one perceives that an injustice has happened, the gracious person does not react impulsively in a fit of rage. We will be wronged or sinned against from time to time by others, but to be gracious requires that one respond to offenses rather than react with intense emotions. When a woman caught in the very act of adultery was brought to Jesus, He first dealt with her wicked accusers in a gracious way and then, treated her graciously.

Jesus also taught how his followers should treat others when he said, *"Do unto others as you would have them do unto you."* (Luke 6:31 KJV) I don't believe I have ever desired another person to treat me with disgrace. I have witnessed political candidates running for public office fall prey to the temptation to minimize their own mistakes while amplifying the wrong doing of others. Several years ago I was watching such a campaign unfold. Speaking in reference to an opponent who had experimented with smoking marijuana in his youth years earlier, a candidate said, "this proves my opponent is morally bankrupt in every conceivable way!" Just a few days later, speaking of his own use of marijuana in his high school days, this same candidate who had been so harsh in his comments to his opponent referred to his own pot use as simply "youthful indiscretion." While it may be natural to minimize our own mistakes while exaggerating the mistakes of others, to the one who has a healthy fear of the Lord, being gracious in relationships becomes the order of the day.

Another time in which our Lord expressed graciousness was as He entered the Garden of Gethsemane. He had instructed his inner circle of disciples, namely Peter, James and John, to stay and pray on His behalf as He went further into the garden alone. He returned to them and found them asleep at a time when He very much needed His friends to be praying for Him. He was gracious in his rebuke to them when he expressed that their *"...spirit is willing but the flesh is weak."* (Matthew 26:41) He was acknowledging something positive about them in the midst of their shortcomings. This event reveals that Jesus was gracious during the times of most tremendous trials in his life. He remains the greatest example of how to be gracious to others not just during good times but also during difficult times.

I have a friend who lost his mother suddenly to a stroke several years ago. Following the funeral, he received a call from a local real estate agent who indicated she had enjoyed a close and enduring love for my friend's mother. She went on to indicate that should he need to sell his mother's place at some point in the future, she would be happy to help the family in any way possible. After a few months, my friend decided to enlist this realtor's help in attempting to determine the fair market value of the home and acreage upon which it was located. This lady who had previously offered her assistance began to curse and hurl profanities at my friend who had lost his mother. Instead of taking offense, he offered to pay twice the usual and customary costs for the realtor's time if she were still willing to help with his research. By the end of that conversation, the realtor was expressing sorrow over her vulgar behavior and sharing how she was still grieving the loss of her own mother a year earlier. My friend, having embraced the healthy fear of the Lord, found it natural to be gracious with another even if the other person was mean spirited and unjust to him. In doing so, the irreverent real estate agent actually responded well to the grace shown to her and dramatically softened her demeanor. While this positive ending does not happen each time one is gracious to another, being gracious certainly increases the likelihood that the offending party will begin to be less offensive.

Being Truthful in Relationships

Since Jesus came as one full of grace and truth, it would make sense that the authentic follower of Christ would stress honesty and truthfulness in his or her relationships. The quality of honesty is particularly important to the heart of God, in that it clearly sets Him apart from His adversary, the devil. The bible says of devil that *"...he is the father of lies."* (John 8:44 NIV) Jesus often stressed the importance of believing and walking in the truth. Someone has rightly observed that the level of satisfaction within a relationship will never rise above the level of truthfulness within that relationship. Few things do more damage within a relationship than that of deception. In working with many marital couples whose relationships were marked by an adulterous affair, I have discovered a frequently occurring phenomenon. While the realization of the sexual unfaithfulness was extraordinarily painful to the betrayed party, the deception of the offending party that was used to conceal the affair, for many, became the greatest hurdle through which to navigate. I have heard time and time again, "if he had been honest when I first raised the issue, it would be so much easier to trust him again. Having lied to me repeatedly before, it's hard to trust him with anything he says anymore."

> **Few things do more damage within a relationship than that of deception.**

Years ago in trying to define various types of dishonesty to Ben, my young son, I shared with him deception can come in different forms. Of course, the most obvious one is seen when someone simply says something that, at its core, is not true. The young lad who says he cleaned up his room as instructed who has yet to enter the room is simply not telling the truth.

Exaggeration of the facts is also a way of being deceptive. If a mother says to her daughter, "if I have told you once I have told you a thousand times tonight, "get into the shower," she has not spoken the truth by having employed exaggeration. I believe it is also possible to misrepresent the truth by remaining silent. For example, if two other people are sharing information and you know facts beyond what they know, and, by remaining silent, they believe a falsehood, you have deceived them by not correcting their inaccurate perspectives. To the one who maintains a reverent and accurately understood fear of the Lord, honesty within relationships becomes common place.

Being Courageous in Relationships

It has been suggested that the most frequently documented quote spoken by Jesus recorded in the Bible is, "Don't be afraid." Perhaps Jesus emphasized the importance of being courageous for at least two reasons. First, apparently we, in the human condition, are highly susceptible to experiencing a myriad of fears. Secondly, when the human heart is gripped by unhealthy fears, that person tends to find himself or herself going further down a road he or she had no business being on in the first place. Five of the most common fears experienced by man were previously mentioned in chapter 2 of this book. Let me simply suggest for our purposes here, that when a person lacks courage in the context of relationships, he or she will allow unhealthy fears to have a negative impact on his or her relationships. To be clear, being courageous is not to be equated with fearlessness. Quite the contrary, fears must be present in order for courage to exist. Courage is not the absence of fear but rather the willingness to face the fear head on.

I recently spoke with a young lady who had been dating a young man for over four years. She had reached a point where she believed the relationship had become emotionally abusive and it was taking a toll on her physical, emotional, and spiritual health. As she unveiled her dilemma, it seemed as if he had made several foolish financial decisions against her counsel. When the negative consequences for his poor decisions began to crash in on him, he asked her to get into her savings and bail him out. She indicated to me that she had helped him out financially several times throughout their relationship in spite of the fact that his monthly income was twice her income. She was afraid that he would be irate with her should she choose to not help as she had done in the past. And yet, it didn't seem right to her to continue paying the price for his poor choices. I encouraged her to love him enough to not assist him this time, and to be courageous enough to risk his anger. While Galatians 6:2 encourages us to help others with their burdens, verse 5 tells us *"for each one should carry their own load."* (NIV) This young lady was struggling to recognize the difference between her boyfriend's burdens and his loads. The term load carries with it the idea of personal responsibility. Ironically, as this young lady chose to keep her hands off that for which her boyfriend was responsible, he accused her of being exceedingly selfish. She elected to be courageous and face his anger as a result of allowing him to harvest from the seed that he had sown. When I last spoke with her, it appeared that she was going to create some time and space in her relationship with her boyfriend, sensing that he may have used her more than actually loved her. While knowing the truth may set a person free, it can sometimes bring with it a measure of pain. I must say, when I encountered her later, her countenance seemed brighter and relief seemed to be the result of her exercising courage within her relationship.

It takes courage to follow Jesus' example of how to be in relationship with others. Whether going against man made social rules by visiting with a Samaritan woman in a public place, or rebuking religious leaders who were choosing to refuse to believe that He was the Messiah prophesied from days of old, Jesus was exceedingly courageous. Nowhere is His courage more clearly on display than when He finishes praying to his Father in the garden. Having begged his Father to release him from needing to drink of the cup of suffering, the Bible states of Jesus in John 18:4-5, *"Jesus, knowing all that was going to happen to him, went out and asked them, 'Who is it you want?' 'Jesus of Nazareth', they replied. 'I am he', Jesus said."* (NIV) The Bible goes on to indicate that when he had spoken, they drew back and fell to the ground. As previously discussed, Jesus very much epitomized what it means to be infused with the healthy and righteous fear of the Lord. It was the fear of his Father in the garden that empowered him to turn and stare death in the face. As a result, he approached his enemies, including the betrayer, and turns himself over to them. In doing so, they fell to the ground. It seems clear that those with a healthy fear of the Lord display courage in the context of their relationship with others.

Being Gentle in Relationships

My adult son along with my wife know full well that I am a stickler for details, particularly in the area of communication. I never cease to be amazed at how two individuals can have a conversation related to a particular topic, and come away with quite different meanings as to what was said. For example, years ago, my wife Rhonda, asked if I wanted to use our vacation time during the upcoming summer to go visit her family in Ohio. After a long pause, I said, "I would be willing to go see your folks this summer." In a bit of a huff, she asked, "What did my folks do to cause you to not want to spend time with them?" Puzzled by her reaction, I let her know that they had never done anything to cause me to not want to go see them and repeated my willingness to go. She said, "That's just it. Your pause tells me you had to wrestle with the decision. Additionally, and I asked if you 'wanted to go see them?' You said, 'I am willing to go see them.' That lets me know that you really don't want to!" In my defense, the pause was me running through my mind what I would need to do to clear my calendar by canceling previous commitments in order to make the trip happen. As it pertains to my wording, I sometimes use the words "willing to" and "want to" interchangeably. That apparently is not the case with my beloved wife. Gregory Bateson, an expert in marriage and family counseling observed years ago, "While it is natural for mankind to long to communicate, good effective communication does not come naturally."

Why spend a paragraph on linguistics when this section is designed to deal with being gentle in our relationships? I find that many people use the terms aggressive and assertive as if both have the same positive meaning. I have also seen individuals define assertive in such a way that it had a strong negative connotation. If, in our relationships, we are going to be able to effectively communicate with each other, it will be imperative that the people involved in a communication define words and concepts in a similar way. Otherwise, one may fail to adequately communicate as shown in my example above. While the subject of how best to communicate can be vigorously debated, most experts generally agree that there exists three primary categories or styles of communication. These include aggressive, non-assertive, and assertive communication. In this paradigm, communication is said to be aggressive if the intent of the speaker is to dominate, humiliate, or otherwise hurt the other person. The intent of the non-assertive speaker is to please or keep the other person happy as a result of the communication. A person is said to have an assertive style of communication if he or she speaks honestly about his or her personal thoughts, feelings, and opinions in a direct fashion but also in a manner that takes into account the other person's thoughts, feelings, and opinions. It is here that gentleness plays a significant role in a person's life who has developed an appropriate fear of the Lord.

For our discussion here, gentleness in relationships describes the manner in which one person handles another person in the context of communication. The person who fears the Lord will take seriously the admonitions in scripture related to how we are to treat others. When addressing his readers and encouraging them to be bold in their witness for Christ, Peter says, *"But in your hearts, revere Christ as Lord. Always be prepared to give an answer to anyone who asks you to give the reason for the hope you have. But do this with gentleness and respect"* (I Peter 3:15, NIV). Throughout this particular chapter, Peter has been admonishing his readers to be mindful of their speech and how they interact with others. We see throughout Jesus' life, some people had honest inquiries of Him from a true heart in pursuit of the truth of a matter. Others clearly had unhealthy motives and posed various questions to Him in an attempt to ensnare Him into misspeaking and making a mistake so they could use His words against Him. Whether from a pure heart of inquiry, or an attempt to create problems, Peter appears to emphasis gentleness as altogether appropriate in responding to others who pose questions to us regarding the hope that is within us. Paul encourages Titus to lead others to *"slander no one, to be peaceable and considerate, and always to be gentle toward everyone"* (Titus 3:2, NIV).

It is so difficult to have surging strong powerful negative emotions pulsating through our bodies and yet respond to others with gentleness. While leading a marriage enrichment event several years ago at a church in Oklahoma City, I was sharing of the important difference between me having anger and anger having me. I also indicated that often, whatever my powerful emotions invite me to say, as a follower of Christ, I may want to respond quite differently. One of the participants shared with the group that to do so feels hypocritical, phony, and deceptive. Several were able to voice the same sentiment. The consensus of the group was that we should be transparent, open, and honest, even if it seems insensitive and mean spirited. After all, if that's how a person really thinks and feels, should he or she not have liberty to express it, even if it means harsh tones and forcefulness? We have already mentioned, previously in this chapter, the importance truthfulness plays in relationships as a result of the fear of the Lord manifested in a person's life. However, to value honesty to the exclusion of gentleness, when both are mandated in scripture, is short of trusting God at this word. I recognize that being gentle with my offender when emotionally distraught or upset is beyond my strength alone. I will need to embrace a strong fear of the Lord in order for His will to be realized in this area of my life. If I always do what my strong negative emotions initially invite me to do, I will likely reveal that my emotions have me rather than me having them.

I need to be reminded by God's Spirit that gentleness and self-control, rather than the actions of others, and my subsequent feelings, are deemed in scripture to be more in line with the fruit of the Spirit (Galatians 5:23). I will likely feel hypocritical and a bit fragmented when I restrain from my typical expressions of anger and hurt. In time, with a mindful fear of God, spiritual growth and development along with sanctification, take another step forward. Gentleness can eventually become the norm for us, even when possessing negative emotions when gripped by a wholesome fear of God.

Being Respectful in Relationships

I maintain that an authentic biblical fear of the Lord leads one to show high levels of respect for others in his or her relationships. When Emerson Eggerichs' work, *Love and Respect: The Love She Most Desires; The Respect He Desperately Needs*, first hit the market, many were taken back by his claims. Most people, including those who are not Christians, acknowledge, along with Eggerichs, that unconditional love is the highest and most noble love of all. Yet, most would

Authentic biblical fear of the Lord leads one to show high levels of respect for others...

see respect in quite a different light. I have heard (and have myself believed) that, respect, unlike love, is to be earned and maintained. Most believe it is very much conditional based upon a person and his or her behavior being worthy of respect. In essence, love should be feely given, but respect is to be earned. Eggerichs offers up the notion that just as love should be unconditional, so respect should be. Many will have a hard time incorporating this into their mindset unless given ample reason for doing so. While we have been admonished to "hate the sin but love the sinner", most of us have seldom been directed to "hate the behavior that is not worthy of respect, but respect the person anyway." It appears that this is a message that Eggerichs is seeking to convey. He is not encouraging respect for disrespectful behavior, but rather respect for the individual who behaves badly.

A righteous fear of the Lord will lead us to see what God's word has to say about respect for others. Peter writes, *"Show proper respect to everyone, love the family of believers, fear God, honor the emperor"* (I Peter 2:17 NIV). Isn't it interesting that Peter includes in this brief verse, four various imperatives. It is not simply a coincidence that the fear of God is one of the four and that respect for everyone is mentioned. Notice how all inclusive respect is to be. Perhaps Peter, being personally commissioned to be an evangelist to the gentiles, learned the hard way that God intends his followers to respect everyone. If you recall, Peter had a vision, using non-kosher food as a metaphor for God's call to evangelize the gentiles. Though he quickly obeyed, at one point, he fears the religious Jewish leaders and pushes away from his mission field. Paul would eventually hear of Peter's fear of man and rebuke him. By the time Peter pens down his encouragement to his readers recorded in scripture, he has renewed his respect for and commitment to the gentiles. This, no doubt, was empowered by his mindful fear of the Lord.

Paul shares his heart to his friends at Philippi by directing them to *"Do nothing out of selfish ambition or vain conceit, but rather, in humility, value others above yourselves. Look not only to your own interests but also to the interests of others."* (Philippians 2:3-4 NIV) In providing counsel to clients who are struggling in their relationships, I encourage them to show respect to others by acknowledging and accepting something that has proven beneficial to me. Namely, that God grants to everyone what I refer to as five fundamental freedoms/responsibilities. God grants to everyone (1) freedom to have thoughts, (2) freedom to perceive, (3) freedom to feel, (4) freedom to choose, and (5) freedom to dream. For those of you who have parented teenagers, you likely have had the opportunity to remind them that with freedom comes responsibility. These five freedoms are also responsibilities that we each have. When I avoid attempting to strip others of these freedoms, I am showing them respect. When I accept my responsibility to exercise these freedoms and not burden others to exercise these for me, I am also showing them respect. I may have a responsibility for inviting others to consider my thoughts, feelings, opinions, and concerns. How they choose to respond to my invitations is their responsibility. I need to respect them as they exercise these freedoms. I may not respect their thoughts, perceptions, feelings, choices, or dreams for their future. But I can respect them as a person and respond to them as God would have me to. Having a valid fear of the Lord will empower me to show respect for others even in the midst of conflict.

In summary, it is my prayer that we all will be responsive to God's desire to cultivate in us a healthy fear of Him, using Christ as our example. Thank you for taking the time to acquaint yourself with this book and may the reality of God's love and grace abound in your life more and more as you put your trust in him.

An Exhortation

Two Crosses, Two Fears

Fear ruled both men. They had been tried and convicted for crimes against the State. Now the terrifying sentence was being meted out in front of everyone who walked past the gruesome scene outside Jerusalem's walls. The physical pain was excruciating, but the rising panic was worse. Dust and blood were thick, but it was the terror that choked them. Since they had no power over their executioners they targeted the man who was dying beside them, screaming at him as though he had sent them to their punishment, hurling abuse at him.

As the tortuous hours passed one of the men experienced a change. Though he was still terrified, the focus of his fear shifted. So when his companion, still driven by the fear of death, railed at Jesus, "Aren't you the Christ? Save yourself and us!" he could not continue to participate in the mockery. The fear of God took center stage in his heart and he rebuked his companion in crime.

"Don't you fear God," he said, "since you are under the same sentence? We are punished justly, for we are getting what our deeds deserve. But this man has done nothing wrong." Then he said, *"Jesus, remember me when you come into your kingdom." Jesus answered him, "I tell you the truth, today you will be with me in paradise"* (Luke 23:39-43 NIV).

One man feared death.
Another feared God.
Both got what they feared.
It is forever true.
We get what we fear.
Fearing God leads us to God.

"It is the LORD of hosts whom you should regard as holy. And He shall be your fear, and He shall be your dread" (Isaiah 8:13).

We have heard the call of God to fear Him. We have examined the promises extended to all who answer that call. Let His purposes now become our passion as we open ourselves to the blessing of the Greater Fear.

Study Questions

Chapter 1: Crossing the Threshold of Courage
1. Describe a time when fear dictated a decision you made, or your motive.
2. Has fear led you to a decision in your life that you now regret?

Chapter 2: The Greater Fear
1. Which of the five common fears have you experienced the most?
2. What will always break the power of a lesser fear in your life?
3. What does man naturally try to do with sin?
4. What does secrecy about your sin cause?

Chapter 3: From God's Heart to Yours
1. At least how many times in the Old and New Testaments do we find explicit statements commending to us the fear of the Lord?
2. In your own words write what the Bible means by "the fear of the Lord."
3. Does the fear of the Lord attract us to Him, or keep us at a distance?
4. Which of the five facets of holy fear have you personally experienced?

Chapter 4: The One Who Showed the Way

1. Do you think the followers of Christ experienced love for Him and at the same time feared Him?
2. Describe a time when the activity of God caused you awe.
3. Isaiah 11:3 states that the Messiah would delight in the fear of the Lord. What is it about fearing God that can evoke delight?

Chapter 5: How We Lost Our Way

1. Have you been unconvinced or unaware of the need to fear the Lord? Which, if any, of the eight reasons listed may have influenced your attitude toward the fear of God?
2. Are there healthy fears we should teach our children? Name at least two.
3. Is conformity to traditions in worship a standard for measuring genuine reverence?
4. Does perfect love cast out all fear? See 1 John 4:16-18. If not all fear is cast out, what fear does this reference refer to?

Chapter Six: Unlocking Heaven's Treasure

1. Name three different relationships between the fear of the Lord and wisdom.
2. How is it possible to simultaneously experience fear of God and the positive benefits of being in

relationship with Him?

Chapter Seven: Reverence in Our Hearts
1. Briefly explain how the fear of the Lord is more than an emotion.
2. Are there actions you have taken, or commitments you have made, that demonstrate reverence for God?
3. In what ways could holiness be perfected in your life? What part can holy fear play in that process?

Chapter Eight: Reverence in Our Homes
1. How does submission to God affect a person's attitude toward submitting to his or her spouse?
2. Will teaching the fear of God harm our children psychologically? How do we know?
3. What will God do for the children of them that fear Him?

Chapter Nine: Reverence in the Church
1. In your experience how much do churches actively cultivate a healthy fear of God?
2. How do some churches promote an unhealthy kind of fear?
3. Does genuine reverence within the church attract or repel people outside the church? What effect does irreverence in the church have on them?

4. Name an area in your church where there is a need for an increased fear of God.

Chapter Ten: Reverence in the Workplace

1. Describe a time when reverence or the lack of it made a difference in the quality of your work.
2. How does the fear of God qualify you for career advancement?
3. Do you have an employer/employee relationship at work that needs the healthy fear of the Lord? How would reverence improve the relationship?

Chapter Eleven: Reverence in Our Relationships

1. How does possessing a healthy fear of the Lord lead to trusting Him more?
2. Of the following qualities: graciousness, truthfulness, courage, gentleness, and respect, which comes most easily for you in relationships when conflict arises? Which of these seems more difficult for you to show when conflict marks one of your relationships?
3. Do you agree with Gary Smalley when he says, "Life is relationships, the rest is just details."? Why or why not.

Made in the USA
Lexington, KY
22 January 2019